Field Guide to a New Species

Field Guide to a New Species

a new, sustainable way to be human

Frederick Timm

Copyright © 2016 by Frederick Timm.

Cover photo by Jay Crane

Library of Congress Control Number:		2016903266
ISBN:	Hardcover	978-1-5144-7082-4
	Softcover	978-1-5144-7081-7
	eBook	978-1-5144-7080-0

All rights reserved. No part of this book may be reproduced or transmitted in any form or by any means, electronic or mechanical, including photocopying, recording, or by any information storage and retrieval system, without permission in writing from the copyright owner.

Print information available on the last page.

Rev. date: 03/08/2016

To order additional copies of this book, contact:
Xlibris
1-888-795-4274
www.Xlibris.com
Orders@Xlibris.com

Table of Contents

Introduction vii

A Description of the Four Types of Humans xi

Acknowledgments xv

Chapter 1: The Beginning of Life 1

Chapter 2: Our Animal Nature: Sex, Sexuality and Attachment 17

Chapter 3: Our Animal Nature: Power 31

Chapter 4: The Middle of Life: Crisis and Integration 43

Chapter 5: The Interface of Ethics and Society 61

Chapter 6: Our Relationship with Oneness 77

Chapter 7: The End of Life 89

Conclusion 105

Introduction

It is understandable that bacteria, a primitive life form, might devour their host and destroy their own lives in the process. But when humanity, the most conscious and evolved species ever to inhabit the planet, devours and destroys its host—the earth—we must stop and question this act of suicide.

As in any suicide, we look for a hidden motive. Why would someone choose to end his or her life? What can't a person face that would compel him or her to do this? Collectively we must ask this same question. What secret is too painful for our common humanity to admit and buried so deep in the collective unconscious that we ignore the horrifying, global symptoms of ecological and economic collapse that threaten our existence? What are we denying? Who are we protecting? Why do we court our own extinction?

Parental and Ancestral Failure

The answer is simple but hard to face. Our parents failed us, hurt us and traumatized us, replicating how their parents and ancestors failed, hurt and traumatized them. This is the secret so difficult for us to face as individuals and, collectively, as a species. Our whole species suffers from trauma and many would rather die than admit this tragic legacy.

It is heartbreaking to realize that our first loves, mother and father, betrayed us when we were vulnerable children under their care. Only an autonomous adult can admit and heal this heartrending reality. Most people don't. Most have children instead and pass on this legacy of trauma to the next generation. It is because of this that we humans are ruled by trauma, not truth.

This phenomenon is not limited to any culture, race or ethnicity—and nowadays even sexual orientation—but is a global compulsion. In fact, having children is the opiate of the masses and the primary way to avoid facing our inner world and healing our traumatic legacy. Hence our species has created an overpopulated, violent and unsustainable world.

What to do?

Many of us see humanity's destructive ways and are appalled. But the ideas needed to change society, even ourselves, seem beyond us. We see the problem but don't know the solution. Therefore, it's good to have a field guide to help us understand why we behave so destructively and to teach us a new way that will not only sustain us globally but fulfill us personally.

Why a field guide?

A field guide is a handy way to identify and learn things about a species in its habitat and to understand its behavior, growth processes, life cycle and survivability. In this field guide, the two species identified are both human and share a habitat—our planet home, Earth. The species are *Homo sapiens*, which have been around for the last seventy thousand years or so, and *Homo veritas*, which are just evolving into being. This guide identifies two intermediate types of human as well, *Rebels* and *Seekers*, both of which are also described in detail.

In essence this field guide delineates four categories of human beings, each in a different place along the evolutionary path to consciousness. The guide investigates how trauma and truth affect the behavior and attitudes of these four types throughout a maturational process that roughly parallels the life cycle. By studying how each type responds to the developmental stages of life's progression as well as different facets of general living, we can assess ourselves and our degree of maturity, both as individuals and a species. We see who will evolve and survive—and who won't and why.

This field guide illustrates something that we as a species sorely lack: a perspective on our behavior and, more deeply, an understanding of our life's purpose—our reason for being.

Hope for a new species

This is a book of hope. Suffused throughout these pages is the message that truth and nature are stronger than the lies of troubled humanity. Some of us are awakening to this reality, this new way of being. We are becoming increasingly conscious of and consonant with truth and nature. We are becoming *Homo veritas* at last. Living this higher way sends a ripple through the universe that affects the unconscious masses and evolution's course. One thing we have learned is that it only takes a few to change the world.

A Description of the Four Types of Humans

Here are the four types of humans, from the least to the most evolved:

Homo sapiens

> The least evolved and currently most common type of human is *Homo sapiens*. Not self-aware, *Homo sapiens* lead unconscious lives. They are the average person. Ruled by trauma, not truth, they number in the billions. They are profoundly wounded by ancestral trauma, which they deny. They shun their inner world and form a fragmented identity, a false self, by conforming to socially-defined roles and rules. They live primarily for comfort. Collectively, they are rapacious, violent and destructive to life. Although human, they lack humanity.

Rebels

> The second type of human, *Rebels*, is transitional. They have begun the process of evolving from trauma to truth and live in the discomfort of knowing too much to fit in yet never enough to grow in a concerted way. They rebel against the strictures of conventional society and the conformity of their unconscious families. They are reactive to the norm, but not proactive in finding something new. As their focus is on those against whom they rebel, they do not investigate their inner world, which also leaves them fragmented within. They are social outcasts, but fail to use this to make a decided forward leap.

Seekers

The third type of human is *Seekers*. *Seekers* have mutated beyond reactive rebellion into proactive self-investigation. They begin to look within to resolve their legacy of childhood trauma and release their magnificence. Although still somewhat fragmented, they are becoming integrated within. They focus their energy on healing and becoming the people they were meant to be. *Seekers* begin the process of evolving into the fourth type of human, *Homo veritas*. It is worth stating that I am a *Seeker*.

Homo veritas

Homo veritas are trauma-free and ruled by truth. They have worked through the wounds of their past and resolved them. No longer fragmented by trauma, they are integrated people. They embody their individual gifts and fulfill a rare purpose of evolving consciousness to the next level of understanding. They affect all they meet and the course of life itself. Living in harmony with nature and all living things, they are the hope for our sustainability on this planet. In such a troubled world as ours, *Homo veritas* are presently more an ideal than a reality—though it needn't be this way in the future.

Different sides of us can be all of these types at the same time

As individuals we are complex. Different sides of us can simultaneously be in different and seemingly contradictory stages of psychic or emotional evolution. Sometimes people who seem to fall clearly into the *Homo sapiens* category can have areas in their lives in which they have great insight and might seem more clearly to be *Homo veritas*. Other people who fall into the category of *Seekers* might have a stuck side that seems more like a *Homo sapiens*. This is to be expected. Similarly, we've all had moments when the clouds parted and the wonder and truth of life broke through. This is how we know our potential—and know that the possibility of becoming *Homo veritas* is real and not an unattainable ideal.

One final thought

Some people are just born different. They are born with more capacity, more rebellion, more awareness, more insight. They were born with more light and more fight—to break away from the deadness of their families and the norm and to struggle out of the deadness of the unresolved traumas within them. As I see it, humanity's future rests upon the shoulders of these people. This book is addressed to them—to bolster their courage as they evolve into a new way.

Acknowledgments

I want to give special thanks to Daniel Mackler, Mark Byfield and Norman F. Ader. Their wise counsel and caring friendship have made writing this book, and its lonely venture into truth, bearable, possible—wonderful.

I would also like to thank the people I have worked with as a therapist. All gave me pieces of the puzzle to inform my understanding of the diverse mosaic of our human story. And to those who ventured into the maze of childhood despair to reveal their dark story and repressed splendor, I give special thanks. It has been a privilege to witness their grief at their painful and at times horrifying history of childhood betrayal. Equally powerful and awe-inspiring was witnessing their wonder as their hope in life emerged and their gifts and talents manifested. Knowing these courageous souls and witnessing their tragic and healed stories, I have walked away blessed and more healed myself. This book is dedicated to them and any who dare to emancipate their inner child into its magnificence.

Chapter 1

The Beginning of Life

At conception, life endows each of us with the seed of a true self. This seed is our original perfection and inviolate. It holds the template for the best of us and the future map for our purpose—and has the potential to be developed throughout our lives. The human capacity to interface with truth through the true self makes human nature the best part of nature—and sacred. Yet for so many people this potential gets blocked. Trauma, especially trauma in childhood, locks humanity out of its perfection, stunts our potential and warps us into something less than sacred. Yet always, beneath the imperfections, the seed of the true self remains, waiting to be reclaimed and developed.

- The Inner Child
- Recalling Childhood
- Our Emotional Age
- The Origin of Trauma
- Truth
- The True and False Self
- Our Purpose and Life's Purpose

The Inner Child

The inner child, analogous to the underdeveloped true self, is the still-alive child part of us that never fully developed into adulthood. For one reason or another it was stunted in our early years and was not entirely able to express its pain, hurt, anger and also magnificence—its gifts. The inner child of the four types of humans expresses itself in the following ways:

***Homo sapiens*—seeking rescue and revenge**

> *Homo sapiens* are unconscious of their inner child—and their inner child is powerful. It was badly hurt in their early years and pulls the puppet strings of their adult personality. Hungry for rescue, the inner child seeks to be loved in the way their real child never was—and believes others have a responsibility to provide it. Also thirsty for revenge against those who hurt it, the inner child now acts this out against convenient stand-ins, usually people who did it no harm and perhaps were not even alive when the actual harm happened.

***Rebels*—blame the norm and parents, try to change them**

> The inner child of *Rebels* is also awash in fantasy of rescue and revenge, however, it blames the norm for its plight—including its normal parents. *Rebels* believe that if only the norm and their parents would change, and often change in relation to one issue, then the inner child's neediness and rage would be quieted. However, this is a fantasy, for if that issue were resolved, then their inner child would simply latch on to a new one.

Seekers—getting in touch, beginning to heal

Seekers have a wounded inner child, but are getting in touch with the dynamics that created its wounds and are gaining awareness about the nature of the people who inflicted them. Through this process they see that their salvation will come not from others changing but from within. This makes them less likely to fall prey to the desire for rescue and revenge, though if they do, they use this as further grist for the mill of self-reflection. That is, they learn from it, grieve their historical losses and become much less likely to repeat it. Also, the more they heal their wounds, the more the gifts of their inner child manifest, leaving *Seekers* increasingly satisfied as adults.

Homo veritas—resolved, manifested

Homo veritas have resolved the wounds of their inner child, which allows their gifts to be freely expressed in their adult life. One might question whether *Homo veritas* have an inner child at all, since their inner child has grown up and integrated with their actual adult. But perhaps it's best to say that their adulthood is now imbued with the innocence of a healthy, free, alive, undamaged, nurtured child—a beautiful ideal for us all.

Recalling Childhood

People recall their childhood in a variety of ways. Some remember none of their childhood, some remember much of their childhood, some remember their childhood in selective or distorted ways and some remember childhood events clearly. The four types of humans recall their childhood as follows:

Homo sapiens—**childhood forgotten or idealized**

> *Homo sapiens* tend to idealize their childhood and forget, minimize or avoid its unsavory parts. However, sometimes there are painful things in childhood—traumatizing events and people—that are too difficult to deny, and they will be remembered, but often as the only bad thing in childhood. The remainder of childhood hurts, or perhaps the context of them, can be idealized or forgotten.

Rebels—**distorted connection with childhood fuels rebellion**

> Although *Rebels* forget or deny much of their childhood history, they often have anger over certain aspects of it, which gives their rebellion a focal point. Other *Rebels* hold on to their unresolved childhood hurts as a new identity: victimhood. *Rebels* can also idealize or distort many of the painful aspects of their childhood, allowing them to remain fundamentally similar to the norm.

Seekers—**studying childhood, gaining empathy for self**

> *Seekers* exhume and explore their childhood history, discovering not just the painful and confusing but the magnificent and wonderful. Through this they relearn the nature of their gifts and also gain empathy for their younger, vulnerable selves. This process opens the door to grieving—the undoing of trauma.

Homo veritas—full awareness of childhood history

Homo veritas have a complete awareness of the truth of their childhood history. They know what they experienced, they recall their feelings, both positive and negative, and they know the nature of the main players of their early life drama. They know what things affected them, they know what their traumas were and they know and have developed their innate gifts. They have nothing to hide from themselves because they are emotionally resolved people.

Our Emotional Age

People have different emotional ages that are often separate from their chronological age. Their emotional age results from their degree of connection with their true selves, their awareness of their childhood history and their connection with life's purpose. The four types of humans have the following emotional ages:

Homo sapiens—children

> Because *Homo sapiens* remain emotionally stuck in childhood, they are slaves to it. They live in older bodies fueled by immature, even infantile, personalities. Because they never developed who they are, their personal evolution stopped long ago.

Rebels—teenagers

> *Rebels* are perpetual teenagers—exploring something new, fighting the norms of their constricted family systems and thinking themselves profoundly different, even though they are only fractionally so. They consider themselves independent adults because of their difference, though they cannot see how they cling to a conforming group of rebellious peers as a new, troubled family system—and identity.

Seekers—young adults

> Emotionally, *Seekers* are young, increasingly independent adults. Because they are learning to stand on their own two feet, they do not so readily need to lean on a social group to define themselves. They still suffer from the wounds of childhood and have to be careful not to regress into childish or teenage behavior when under duress, but they resolve these wounds day by day through the hard work of self-study and grieving. Each day they learn more about the person they once were and the newfound adult they are becoming.

Homo veritas—adults

Homo veritas are mature adults. They live independent lives in thought, emotion and action and are not swayed by the arrows of an uncaring or misguided external world. They know their history through and through but are not slaves to it, having redefined a new future for themselves, which they continue to develop as they walk life's path with eyes wide open.

The Origin of Trauma

What is the origin of trauma, that intense and negative experience that overwhelms our emotional growth process and stunts our development? Is trauma a natural process, an inherent part of being human? Or is it unnatural, unnecessary, even avoidable? It is clear that trauma has a profound effect over almost every aspect of our lives, but it is less clear what people think about its origin. Let us explore how the four types of humans view the origin of trauma.

Homo sapiens—unaware, in denial

Homo sapiens deny the origins of trauma. They label trauma as a part of human nature—as innate, a tragic flaw or even original sin. Some even claim that trauma is necessary for our growth, that it makes us strong. They point out that animals naturally traumatize each other, though they fail to see how we are different from animals—that unlike animals we have higher sides that are more evolved. Also, *Homo sapiens* often do more than deny the origin of trauma: they deny the existence of trauma entirely, and by default its effects.

Rebels—unaware, blame others

Rebels think *Homo sapiens* are the problem. They blame *Homo sapiens* and their conventional ways for the ills of humanity, and, if they consider trauma at all—which many do not—they hold *Homo sapiens* responsible for its origins. At best, since *Rebels* do not self-investigate, they are only aware of a limited slice of the trauma spectrum—because they themselves are so traumatized yet simultaneously unaware of it.

Seekers—inward-looking, questioning

Seekers have woken up to the realization that they are deeply traumatized and begin to question the origins of trauma. The more they look within and study their inner terrain and family history, the more they realize that their whole family is traumatized, their ancestors were traumatized and that everyone's ancestors and the whole sweep of our human family were traumatized, ad infinitum. They also begin to make the connection between people's unresolved traumas and their compulsion to traumatize others in similar ways.

Homo veritas—aware, grasp full picture

Homo veritas see trauma as a problem with misguided humans, arising from our earliest ancestors. They realize that when we emerged from our evolutionary origins with a large brain, capable of self-reflection, we failed to fulfill what this expanded mental capacity allowed and required. They realize that our transition from instinctive animal to conscious human remains incomplete—that we applied our increased brain capacity to the animal instincts of sex and aggression but not to the more evolved ideals of ethical cooperation and altruistic nurture. They see that this misuse of mind—becoming clever, brutal animals and not wise, cooperative humans—wounded us from the start and is the origin of our trauma.

Truth

Truth is reality. There are four ways we can perceive reality and therefore know truth: through our reason, our emotions, our intuition and our five senses. All four of these ways, however, are susceptible to distortion due to trauma. The four types of humans relate to truth in the following ways:

Homo sapiens—disconnected from truth

> The norm asks, "What is truth?"—because they really don't know. Sometimes they defend against this by believing in false truth with great confidence. Real truth scares them, because it is a wake-up call they wish to avoid. Their four ways of understanding truth have been distorted by trauma and they wish to keep it that way. They misuse their reason to outsmart nature and rationalize their bad behavior. They shun and buffer the range of their emotions. They discredit their intuition as magical or unscientific. And they misuse their bodies, exploiting their five senses to jolt them into feeling alive. Others trivialize and personalize truth by saying it is relative—"my truth" and "your truth." This keeps the profound, universal demands of truth at bay.

Rebels—rebellion mistaken for truth

> *Rebels* are angry at the untruth of the norm but end up, in their reactivity, following a different version of untruth. They sense correctly that their rebellion is more vital than conventional submission, yet they do not pursue further investigation into the meaning of truth. Since they have not resolved their traumas, their reason, emotions, intuition and five senses remain distorted, limiting their understanding of truth, especially inner truth.

Seekers—truth coming into focus

Because *Seekers* have begun to heal their traumas, they open the door to discerning truth. As they grieve their past and emancipate their gifts, their intellect clears, their emotions return, their intuition guides them with greater accuracy and their five senses connect them with awe and delight to their bodies and the natural world. They mutate from the illusions of the past and become grounded in the present, interfacing directly with truth. They realize that truth is their friend.

Homo veritas—living truth

Homo veritas are truth embodied. To them, the question "What is truth?" is moot, because they know there is but one truth and that it flows through them. All four ways of knowing reality operate fully and harmoniously inside them. Not only do they perceive reality accurately through reason, intuition, emotions and the senses, they are reality and are at one with ultimate reality—with truth. For them the mystery of life is resolved, because they are intertwined with it. Fully conscious, they are the answer to the questions of existence.

The True and False Self

Our relationship with the true and false self defines who we are. As we experience trauma in our upbringing, including in the womb, the seed of our true self gets buried in the unconscious and the false self becomes established. A saving grace in childhood, the false self is a defensive mask behind which the seed of the true self remains safe and inviolate, waiting for our reclamation in adulthood. Other factors color our relationship to our true and false self: our inborn capacity for authenticity, our motivation to be real and the growth opportunities provided by our environment. The four types of humans relate to the true and false self as follows:

Homo sapiens—true self buried, false self established

> *Homo sapiens* bury the seed of their true self in the unconscious and build a false self for protection. Surrounded by a troubled family and society, they forget that their true self ever existed and think the false self is the only self. Their true self remains buried for a lifetime—and they label this state normal and appropriate.

Rebels—seed of true self erupts

> In *Rebels*, the seed of the true self erupts, causing them to rebel against the corrupt traditions of the norm's false self. However, they are unconscious of the meaning of their rebellion, because they do not self-investigate. Their focus remains outward. They do not realize that they are also living through a false self—of reactivity.

Seekers—true self nurtured

Seekers sense the power and potential of the true self. No longer so reactive, they struggle to avoid getting locked in battle with those who refuse to grow. Instead, they shift their focus to internal healing and self-nurture. With a ferocity they refuse to deaden, they embrace the undertaking of self-discovery. As they resolve their traumas and dismantle the false self, their true self emerges as central to their being.

Homo veritas—true self embodied

Homo veritas are consonant with their true self. Having resolved their traumatic legacy, they have no false self nor any need for one. They live in synch with truth and their true self becomes a beacon for all to see.

Our Purpose and Life's Purpose

Our purpose is the thing that calls us forward. It helps us decide how to spend our day, with whom to associate, what to strive for, what to avoid, what dreams to aspire to and what goals to hold dear. People's purposes in life can be complex and varied. Life's purpose, on the other hand, is simple: to evolve into consciousness—to know itself through its evolving creation. The degree to which we as individuals and a collective whole have a purpose that is consonant with life's purpose depends on our connection with our true self, as follows:

Homo sapiens—**conform to false purposes**

> Since *Homo sapiens* live through a false self, they are disconnected from life's purpose. They instead construct false purposes to which they strive to conform, no matter how dysfunctional or destructive. Some of these include entering unconscious relationships, having children, working disconnected jobs, amassing money and resources and living for comfort. Their goals in life are defined by conformity to familial roles and cultural rules.

Rebels—**rebel against convention**

> *Rebels'* purpose is to engage in endless rebellion, defying their family's unconscious, destructive patterns and exposing the corrupt compromises of the conventional world. However, this purpose is also corrupt, because its reactivity denies them a proactive, conscious connection to the true self.

Seekers—mutate into something new

Seekers look within and realize that their true purpose is deeper than anything they previously imagined. No matter the price or social opprobrium, they live to do the inner work of dismantling the false self and aligning with truth. They do this by healing their traumas and freeing their gifts. They live for a proactive purpose which fulfills them as they mutate into something new.

Homo veritas—evolve consciousness

Homo veritas' purpose and life's purpose are one—to evolve consciousness, expand its meaning and inspire. This honors their covenant with life. Aligned with their true self, they are optimally equipped to fulfill evolution's quest to evolve life into the sacred.

Chapter 2

Our Animal Nature: Sex, Sexuality and Attachment

In the mists of time, humans emerged with a large brain capable of self-reflection. However, certain aspects of our lives—namely sex and power—are still based on an animal template. In this chapter we explore the sexual side: sex, sexuality and issues around attachment that lead to family life. These have a biological foundation, yet express themselves in profoundly different ways depending on our degree of psychological development. We have the capacity to imbue our animal nature with ideals, a level of insight and evolved behavior that no other animal has. But how do we live up to these ideals? And in what ways do we fall short, and why?

- Sexual Energy and Sex
- Romantic Love
- Celibacy
- Becoming Parents
- Family of Origin
- The Family System We Create

Sexual Energy and Sex

Sexual energy is powerful. It carries a desire for union and procreation—and also for creative expression and reverence for the beauty and wonder of life. To one degree or other it flows through all of us. It is part of our biology, but when expressed through the complex matrix of our personalities it carries other dimensions—glorious or disastrous. After all, sex is simple, we're not. The four types of humans relate to sexual energy and sex in the following ways:

Homo sapiens—sex for procreation and acting out

Homo sapiens' wounded inner child is so focused on dynamics of rescue and revenge that it cannot help but commandeer the sex drive for these purposes. The norm, realizing the ill effects of this, often tries to restrict sex to monogamous relationships with an ultimate goal of procreation. But for so many, the hurt inner child is too rapacious for that, leaking out sexual energy through all sorts of secret outlets such as lust, pornography, compulsive masturbation, promiscuity, infidelity and sadomasochism, to name a few. Although the norm tends to frown upon these outlets, it tacitly approves of them, as engaging in them is less painful and more protective of denial than healing the childhood wounds that motivate them.

Rebels—wild sex, rebellious procreation

Freed of the norm's repressive rules, *Rebels* use sex without restraint, even recreationally. They act out sexually in similar ways to *Homo sapiens*—pornography, promiscuity, sadomasochism and the like—but openly, even proudly as part of their so-called emancipation. They feel they are a sexual step ahead of the norm, and in a sense they are, because there is some truth to the notion that we are only as sick as our secrets. However, they still fail to explore what they are acting out—the inner child's unmet needs and wounds. Although some rebel against the norm by not having children, others do have children, and without preparation, naively thinking their liberated stance will make them better parents than their own.

Seekers—studying sexual patterns, exploring celibacy

If *Seekers* engage in libertine sexual behavior, they discover emerging patterns. They see they have used sex and sexual energy symbolically to reenact their history of childhood betrayal. As they decode their conduct, they learn more about how they were wounded as children and what needs healing. This is freeing, but with freedom comes responsibility, which is why many *Seekers* engage in periods of celibacy—to discover the deeper nature of sexual energy. Through this exploration they begin to imbue their sexual instinct with the ideals of ethics and altruism.

Homo veritas—conscious sexuality for creative purpose

Homo veritas use sexual energy for creative purposes. The ideals of ethics and altruism fully inspire their sexual instinct. Likewise, their sexual instinct grounds their ideals in human warmth and attachment. If they choose to be sexual with self or another, their sex would be conscious, constructive and also enhancing of self-love and love of the other. In an ideal world, *Homo veritas* would use their sexual energy carefully and, rarely, for procreation—to create a new life bathed in love and nurture. However, in such a troubled world as ours, a preferred choice for many *Homo veritas* is conscious celibacy.

Romantic Love

Romantic love, that passionate emotional yearning for or attachment to another, affects most everyone at some point in their lives. It is a central life goal for many people, a beacon of light on the quest for happiness and meaning and a prelude to a marriage of souls. Yet romance plays out differently for people at different stages of emotional evolution, as follows:

Homo sapiens—rescue fantasy, then revenge

Romantic love for *Homo sapiens* is the wounded inner child's unconscious fantasy of rescue in the arms of the perfect partner—the perfect parent in disguise. Some *Homo sapiens* are so emotionally out of touch that they succeed in maintaining stable, though emotionally limited and self-deceptive, romances. These merged relationships, sometimes ratified as marriages, seal the tomb on the inner child's growth. For many, however, when expectations fall short and the glow of romance fails, revenge begins—the rage and pain of an abandoned child. Others bypass revenge by just trying again, searching for the new and perfect romance—an impossible, never-ending quest that often involves settling for less.

Rebels—free but disconnected relationships

With their liberation from convention, *Rebels* freely explore romance—yet in a disconnected way. Some engage in multiple, open relationships or other unconventional permutations, and in these someone often gets hurt—because they never address the underlying emotional dynamics. Sometimes *Rebels* are able to form long-term relationships, even marriages, but as a rule these are with other *Rebels* who share a common external issue or enemy. Often these relationships end in breakup or divorce.

Seekers—growing conscious of replicated patterns

Seekers struggle with romantic love, because underneath it they are struggling to love themselves. Many jump from one failed romance and its obsession to the next, learning along the way that the common denominator in this anguish is them. They begin to correlate the heartbreak and unrequited love of the present with that which they experienced as children with their first loves and first betrayers—mother and father. As they heal this historical tragedy, they become more available to healthy romantic relationships, which often begin as supportive, platonic friendships and follow the trajectory of old-fashioned courtship. Here they establish emotional and spiritual intimacy as a precursor to physical and sexual intimacy.

Homo veritas—true love of self and others

Homo veritas know that true love comes from the true self. They have a love affair with themselves and truth—and are married within. Since their childhood wounds are healed, they no longer look to others to fill the love deficits inflicted by their parents. As adults, they embody the phrase "I am the love of my life." They may form love bonds with others who have done the work of self-healing and now also live in self-love. These new relationships are deeply rewarding, based in mutual aid, honest sharing and true love from the true self of each. Through these bonds, they grow as individuals and as partners into realms unknown.

Celibacy

Celibacy is abstinence from sexual relations, potentially even masturbation. People can be celibate for a variety of reasons, ranging from a purposeful choice to an unwanted default. People can also be celibate for varying lengths of time. People at different stages of emotional evolution approach celibacy in different ways, as follows:

Homo sapiens—celibacy equated with dissociation, repression

> Although some *Homo sapiens* are celibate because they cannot find a partner, others turn to celibacy as a way to avoid the guilt and shame of sexual acting out or to avoid triggering disturbing sexual memories from childhood, such as sexual abuse. For these reasons, celibacy can bring *Homo sapiens* some comfort, though this repression of sexual energy can create distortions in their personality, warps in their social relationships and even motivations to sexually abuse or otherwise violate innocents. It is for these reasons that *Homo sapiens* generally look upon celibacy suspiciously and do not see it as growth-inducing—because for them it is not.

Rebels—celibacy a default option of frustration

> Some *Rebels* default to celibacy out of frustration when they see that their sexual and romantic exploits have failed them. Celibacy now becomes their new discomfort—another source of complaint at an unfair world. For them, celibacy is not a refuge for learning and growth, rather, a cage of loneliness, isolation and deprivation. Many *Rebels* consider celibacy a thing to be tolerated until it can be ended—and use masturbation to help get them through.

Seekers—celibacy a tool for self-knowledge

Seekers, having realized that undisciplined sex never brought them the deeper happiness or intimacy for which they longed, explore celibacy and even abstinence from masturbation as an opportunity for learning. Celibacy becomes a chance to see what contained sexual energy might reveal. Often it shines a light on their sexual history, including childhood sexual confusion and abuse. This provides a golden opportunity for healing—and more. Miraculously, the life-endorsing, creative nature of sexual energy begins to flow through them, inspiring a deeper understanding of sex beyond overt expression and orgasm.

Homo veritas—celibacy a normal, healthy state

Celibacy is a normal, healthy state for *Homo veritas.* Overt sex tends to hold less appeal to them than the creative, loving potency of a more transcendent sexuality that now emerges from within them. Contained sexual energy imbues all aspects of their lives, grounding their higher purpose in warmth, meaning and compassion. In total celibacy they become lovers of life in a potent and transforming way.

Becoming Parents

People have children for a variety of reasons, from the biological to the psychological. Their quality as parents varies significantly, depending upon their degree of emotional evolution. The four types of humans have children for the following reasons and function as parents in the following ways:

Homo sapiens—birth children to avoid healing inner child

> *Homo sapiens* have children to avoid giving birth to their wounded inner child. The child they create buffers them like a drug from their denied traumatic past. They expect the child to rescue them and project their failed dreams onto the child, hoping its vitality will restore meaning to their lives. They act out their denied rage on the child through violence or indifference, both of which are easy to do because the child lives at their disposal. They resent the life before them, as it confronts their own deadened potential. Conversely, some parents spoil their child to make up for their own childhood deficits. But a spoiled child is not a loved child—and becomes wounded by excesses that lack the reality of true love and true limits.

Rebels—think they'll be better parents, but aren't

> Liberated from conventional restraints, *Rebels* think their freewheeling attitude is the answer to good parenting. They think they will avoid the pitfalls of a troubled society and do better than their repressive parents, but they don't—and can't. Until the wounds of their past are healed, *Rebels* inflict them on their own children. Sometimes their abuse is overt and sometimes it expresses itself in neglect of the child's real needs. However, these dynamics are impossible for *Rebels* to see, as they remain invested in believing themselves advanced and healed.

Seekers—birth their inner child, parent themselves

Seekers are self-aware enough to know that they have no business having children—because they know their unresolved wounds render them unfit. They also see what a troubled world we live in and don't want to bring children into it. Instead they focus on parenting themselves—and birthing their inner child. However, some had children before they became *Seekers*—and know they made a mistake. While raising their children they work to heal their wounds in order to amend this error and inflict as little harm as possible.

Homo veritas—parent the wounded masses

Homo veritas abstain from having children, even though they would be quality parents. In an ideal world *Homo veritas* would procreate responsibly. However, until that world evolves into being they do not. In an overpopulated, polluted and violent world, more children are not needed—enlightened parental figures are. With an inner child who has matured into a self-actualized adult, *Homo veritas* take on a parental role in the world. They parent the lost masses, all of whom are wounded children needing wise, nurturing, ethical guides.

Family of Origin

Everyone has a different relationship with his or her family of origin—from close to distant, from harmonious to contentious. The four types of humans relate to their families of origin in the following ways:

Homo sapiens—close with family

> *Homo sapiens* tend to be close with their families of origin. They criticize them minimally and generally consider them healthy and normal—because they are like them. They love and honor their parents—which mirrors the degree to which they misunderstand the meaning of love and honor. Many stand for "family first" and are skeptical of others who have conflicted or estranged family relationships. In an attempt to retain the troubled harmony of their family systems, they are quick to undermine members who step outside the accepted bounds of normalcy.

Rebels—rebel from family, but only on surface

> *Rebels* find ways to break from their families of origin, rebel against them, even vilify them. They see themselves as different from their families, yet are more like them than they realize. Often they hold much anger toward their families, resentment even, yet lack a nuanced understanding of what their families did to them. Thus their rebellion only simmers on the surface. Some *Rebels* break from their families in select ways, yet stay close with them in others.

Seekers—breaking from the family

Seekers flee the family and from a distance explore its dynamics and their relationship with its members. They come to see the average family as a closed system, a cult—and the basis of all cults. As this exploration continues they become aware of the profound tragedy of their origin. This leads them into a prolonged mourning process. They increasingly feel their full range of pain, anger and sorrow. Meanwhile, they may return to their family to see if it has changed—and also how they have changed.

Homo veritas—broken from their family

Homo veritas are fully broken from their families of origin—yet healed from the familial damage done to them. They understand their family history, including their ancestors' histories, and understand the full nature of the intergenerational cycle of trauma. They also understand the nature of the individual members of their families, though this does not necessarily mean they are drawn to them or have regular contact with them, especially if their families remain wedded to being closed.

The Family System We Create

Family is our most intimate place of bonding, security and safety—and most importantly, the setting for our childhood development. When we become chronological adults, what type of family systems do we create for ourselves? Different people at different levels of emotional evolution create different types of family units, as follows:

Homo sapiens—family as cult

> The family of *Homo sapiens* is a cult. They honor neither the sacred trust of childrearing nor the child's curiosity about life's potential beyond the family. Instead, they indoctrinate the child's mind, kill curiosity and foster dependency on the family. Any thorough evaluation of family life is reviled since it might reveal the cruelty that has been hidden for generations. Their goal is to idealize the parents and ancestors and place blame for their crimes on the Other. Collectively, these insular families become nations and religions that idealize national heroes and time-honored saints and vilify menacing outsiders, be they imagined or real. Children or adults who dare critique this system are shunned.

Rebels—alternative cults based on common rebellion

> *Rebels* break from the family cult to form another cult—based on external rebellion. They band together with others around family ejection and social injustice. These new family units, which may include spouses and children, are based on fighting for similar causes and against similar enemies. They punish those who question their new norms, just as they were punished by their childhood families of origin.

Seekers—kindred souls seeking truth

Seekers find allies, others who have left their families of origin, and join with them to create something new. No longer alone in their wilderness journey, they grow close with their new kinfolk in order to foster, not destroy, what is true within. They realize that these families of spirit are not intended to be places to raise children or fight the world, rather, to grieve, birth the stifled inner child and nurture growth.

Homo veritas—the human family

Homo veritas recognize that all people, whatever their level of development, are one family. They see that all of humanity is interconnected—that all belong to each other and to all that is. They are like parents of this new family, reaching out to everyone and offering love and kindness and respect to all—but also, like a healthy parent, maintaining limits. Their goal is to help all members of this family evolve to their highest potential.

Chapter 3

Our Animal Nature: Power

The instinctual drive of power is another link to our animal forebears. It grounds us in the struggle of life on Earth and facilitates our physical survival. It is the passion we need to assert ourselves in the world—and defines our right to exist and evolve. Yet when blocked by trauma, our power becomes misdirected and misused, taking on perverse dimensions. Here we explore how humans navigate facets of this most powerful animal energy.

- Personal Power
- Collective Power
- Laws People Create and Follow
- Law Enforcement and Prison
- War

Personal Power

We all have personal power, or at least the potential for it. This is the power to fight for ourselves as individuals and find our unique place in the world. But where does this power come from? And what do we do with its potential? Do we use it for growth and evolution—or stagnation and violence? The four types of humans relate to personal power in the following ways:

Homo sapiens—abnegate personal power

Homo sapiens' power comes from the group—not the self. The norm abnegates personal power and dons the authority of the family and culture with arrogance and grandiosity to compensate for this loss. Through conformity, *Homo sapiens* lose their sense of agency—that awareness that they can change their lives and make a positive difference. Instead, this thwarted power leaks out in ugly and often violent ways, with painful consequences for themselves, their intimates and ultimately society.

Rebels—taste personal power through rebellion

Rebels get a taste of personal power through rebelling against their compromised parents and the conventional world. Their power remains reactive to the limits of the norm and fails to transition into self-investigation and other proactive purposes. Although they can become highly energized around a topic or even victorious in a battle, their lack of inner structure fails to contain their power and inevitably dissipates, leaving them feeling disempowered again and again.

***Seekers*—embrace and increase personal power through self-knowledge**

Seekers maintain a strong if at times tenuous connection to their personal power, which they use to propel them out of the family in order to save their souls. Their personal power protects their developing self from the negating world, so they can explore their gifts and grow. As their self-knowledge increases through introspection and life experience, they become adept at bearing the hardships of the wilderness and use the rage of the wounded child to empower their survival. They also use their personal power to confront and condemn their own internalized, damning voices of mother and father.

***Homo veritas*—personal power is universal power**

For *Homo veritas,* personal power is synonymous with the universal power of truth. Trauma-free, they channel the power of the universe through the true self—impacting the world around them. As a new paradigm of humanity, they motivate and guide others by their ethical and altruistic example. With authority, they defend everyone's true self and individual rights from attack. But most importantly, their personal power motivates them to keep expanding themselves and consciousness itself.

Collective Power

As we form groups and societies, we gather our personal selves into a collective self and amass personal power into collective power. This collective power can be used for various purposes—the just and unjust, the nurturing and violating and the conscious and unconscious, as follows:

***Homo sapiens*—a mob, cult, family, tribe, nation**

> Fueled with collective power, *Homo sapiens* gladly join the mob and its fury and are susceptible to violence and an extreme lack of empathy for those who are different. They displace their rage on external foes, be they fabricated foreign enemies, nearby marginalized minorities or even scapegoats within their own families. Someone else always receives the torrent of their collective, muzzled wrath. They find safety in numbers and courage in the group, be it a sect, tribe, gang, battalion, army, state, nation—or family.

***Rebels*—collective rebellion against the norm**

> *Rebels* use their collective power to correct social ills. Since they have not made the connection between inner trauma and social violation, their answer to social ills involves external fixes and well-meaning surface remedies. But these never solve the problem for long. Conflict erupts again in new forms and the battle begins anew, always with a slightly different face but the same basic essence.

Seekers—union of souls undergoing inner healing

Seekers join together to foster liberation movements to free themselves and others from the internalized ills of the family system. Rather than fight the wrongs of the external world, they create groups and organizations that nurture individual growth and support a union of *Seekers*—because they know all too well how lonely the inner journey can be.

Homo veritas—a conscious community

Homo veritas pool their personal power for public good and in so doing live at the center of a conscious community. Through this they lead others into conscious living and simultaneously expand their own consciousness. They do not hide their talents and light to protect the denial and smallness of a hurt world. Together, they live as an example of humans harnessing the power of truth to empower the best in us all.

Laws People Create and Follow

There are two types of laws as relate to human beings: civil laws and universal laws. Civil laws are the rules that bind society. Universal laws are the rules that bind reality. However, as noted earlier, people at different stages of emotional evolution view reality differently, thus laws differently. Not surprisingly, their social laws reflect this. The four types of humans view laws in the following ways:

Homo sapiens—confused, self-serving laws

> *Homo sapiens* create confused laws based on their own distorted versions of reality. Their laws are self-serving—in the sense that they serve the false self. They believe their laws to be appropriate and universal, though often they are neither. Likewise, they do not enforce their laws equally, as those who create the laws are often least subject to them. Their laws are ultimately intended to maintain the troubled status quo—and are often effective at that, at least in the short-term.

Rebels—new but still confused laws

> *Rebels* create laws based on the realization that the norm's laws are often unjust. They struggle to create new laws, but lacking a universal grounding in reality make laws that are also distorted—not fully aligned with universal law. Their laws, however, often have some improvement over the laws of their forefathers. Also, when faced with unjust laws of the norm, *Rebels* may be willing to break them and even martyr themselves in the process.

Seekers—redefining laws from within

Seekers begin to break the laws of denial and unconscious authority—and the new laws they create reflect this. These laws are rooted in the true self and infused with the power and meaning of ethics and morality. However, *Seekers'* laws still lack some universality, depending on the degree to which their creators have not resolved their own traumas. Also, because of their deepening love for their true selves, *Seekers* are cautious about breaking even the unjust laws of the norm because they have no wish to martyr themselves.

Homo veritas—higher law

Homo veritas embody the laws of the universe. They use these higher principles to define the laws of society and form a new social order based on truth. Their laws are in harmony with the rights of the land and animals and children and plants and all people. They recognize that many people who are not *Homo veritas* rankle at these laws—to the degree that they remain traumatized. But *Homo veritas* do not compromise their expressions of justice for the sake of protecting others' denial.

Law Enforcement and Prison

How do people in society deal with lawbreakers? This opens the topic of law enforcement and prison—the removal of a violator's freedom for the sake of society. Here we look at how social groups at different levels of emotional evolution enforce the laws they have created.

Homo sapiens—prisoners of trauma

As prisoners of childhood trauma, *Homo sapiens* are comfortable with the concept of literal prisons. They lock away those who violate the arbitrary laws they consider sacred. Their goal is to enforce adherence through punishment, which is what their parents did to the healthiest sides of them and what they do to the healthiest sides of their children. They throw people considered extreme lawbreakers into the horror of solitary confinement, since this is where the norm's inner child lives—banished from consciousness. Many are also comfortable with capital punishment, since the inner child of the average lives on death row, if it hasn't already been put to death through denial and neglect.

Rebels—escapees who replicate what was done to them

Rebels are nearly as confident in enforcing their own arbitrary laws as are *Homo sapiens*, with one caveat: as black sheep they know what it's like to be judged unfairly. Yet they remain sheep, having in essence escaped one prison only to enter another. They have no problem punishing breakers of their laws and removing their freedoms—under the guise of societal protection. Meanwhile, they may have escaped some aspects of the prison of their families, but their reactive protests against social injustice and disregard for the norm's rules can end them up in society's prisons.

Seekers—wary enforcers, dismantle their psychic prison

Seekers are wary of prisons because they put so much energy into dismantling the psychic prison into which they were indoctrinated. They are naturally drawn to rehabilitating law offenders—as opposed to punishing them—because their main focus is on rehabilitating themselves. *Seekers* are wary of the power of law enforcement, being humble enough to know that even the laws they have created could harm people.

Homo veritas—peacekeepers, rehabilitate through containment

Homo veritas are a new breed of peacekeeper, since they understand that others' bad behavior is but an expression of a traumatized inner child. They understand that perpetrators are hurt children who need to be stopped, contained and brought to justice, which means being understood, loved and rehabilitated. They also have the creativity to consider options that maximize offenders' freedom both during and after containment in order to give them the best chance to grow, heal and flourish. In essence, *Homo veritas* embody the adage of loving their enemies.

War

War is the embodiment of conflict. War can play out in any number of ways—between groups of people and nations, between individuals in a family, even within the psyche of an individual. People at different stages of evolution relate to these types of war in their own unique ways, as follows:

Homo sapiens—warmongers, take sides

Homo sapiens go eagerly to war as a needed external outlet for the denied fury of their collective inner child. Members of the norm see themselves as good and are blind to their part in conflict to the degree that they are blind to their parents' flaws. Similarly, they see their enemy as bad—thus a justifiable target. The extent to which *Homo sapiens* cannot see the flaws of their parents is the extent to which they cannot see the humanity of their enemies. Meanwhile, the norm may give lip service to wishing for peace and abhorring war, but unconsciously they welcome it—and its accompanying patriotism and mass murder.

Rebels—fighters for narrow causes

Rebels are natural warriors but do not always go to war in the usual sense. Their fights tend to be closer to home. They fight injustice, but do not displace their rage onto the enemies of the norm. Rather, they often identify with the norm's enemies and take their side, sometimes blindly. They charge into protests and resistance movements to bring awareness to the corruption of the average. Yet their fuming lacks a vision of what a new, healed way might be. Thus, their battles are often narrow, lacking the nuance and scope that self-awareness brings.

Seekers—freedom fighters in the battle to heal within

Seekers focus on the internal battle to wrest their soul from the clutches of a traumatizing past. They become true freedom fighters, struggling for their independence as they shine the light on the misdeeds of mother and father and the corrupt social systems that support them. This inner battle supplants their need to make external war. In response to society's warfare and protests, they become conscientious objectors, refusing to participate in senseless violence and unwilling to pay with their spirit. However, they do practice self-defense—because they have a real self to defend.

Homo veritas—peacemakers

For *Homo veritas*, war is over. *Homo veritas* embody peace. Since their inner world is at peace, there is no need for outer violence, protest or war. However, a struggle does continue in their lives: to resolve global trauma, to align the masses with truth and to bring peace to Earth. This is one battle these peace-filled beings wage, and for them it is a battle upwelling from their soul—a fierce battle of living true.

Chapter 4

The Middle of Life: Crisis and Integration

If we fail to integrate our split-off sides, crises emerge at each stage of the life cycle, most notably the midlife crisis. Crises call into question how we're living our lives and demand that we listen. They are our soul's desperate urge to love us and are an opportunity for us to get to know ourselves better, redefine our purpose and live more in harmony with others. The question is, do we integrate these erupting truths or push them further into the unconscious, plodding forward toward the next crisis-to-be?

- The Heart Center
- Midlife Crisis
- Psychosomatic Illness
- Mental Disturbances
- Addictions
- Grieving
- Relationship to Abusers
- Facing Our Collective, Global Catastrophe

The Heart Center

In midlife, we evaluate the health of our heart—the center of our being. Most assess the physical heart, but some, when prompted by crisis, assess the metaphorical heart—the heart center. Does our heart center allow universal love to flow through our being to stimulate our growth and facilitate the integration of the self? The four types of humans relate to the heart center in the following ways:

Homo sapiens—a closed heart

> The heart center of *Homo sapiens* is closed, constricted by trauma. This thwarts love's ability to flow through the body and integrate the self. *Homo sapiens* cannot heal their heart because they live in a bubble of denial, unable to see that it is broken by the misfortunes of their past. But their repressed pain and thwarted love force will not remain silent forever. Often, it manifests in a physical crisis such as a heart attack, which they patch up with surgery and medication—not self-investigation.

Rebels—a broken heart

> *Rebels* know their heart is broken, but do not understand why. They are in a perpetual crisis of heartbreak, because they cannot look within to discover the source of their anguish—childhood despair. They live in low-grade suffering, blaming external sources for their misery and remaining perpetually reactive to them.

Seekers—a healing heart

Seekers in crisis experience breakdown—but relinquish their defenses and admit that their heart is broken. Having taken this humbling step, they begin to wonder why. Through self-reflection, they trace its source to the tragedy of their childhood. Their breakdown now becomes a breakthrough, a window into their tragic past—and they begin to heal through a grief process. Their broken heart becomes a broken-open heart, letting in love and understanding.

Homo veritas—an open heart

Homo veritas live crisis-free—with an open heart. Love flows freely through their heart center, infusing their being and transforming them and the world around them. They have boundaries to protect their sacred nature and profound vulnerability. A shield of light keeps them safely open in a corrupt world. This open-hearted approach threatens some, who try to destroy it and bring it back to darkness. Others are drawn to it—and bask in its warmth.

Midlife Crisis

The midlife crisis is unique, because it comes at a time when we are old enough to see unproductive patterns yet young enough to fix them. It can hit us in our twenties, thirties, forties or beyond—striking both women and men, and for a variety of reasons. The four types of humans relate to midlife crises in the following ways:

***Homo sapiens*—midlife crisis ignored, opportunities scorned**

> In fleeting moments of midlife honesty, *Homo sapiens* admit that meaning has drained out of their lives and functioning has become hard. The daily drama and family turmoil they have long relished as diversion no longer protect them from the real crisis in their lives—the tragedy of their childhood. They feel something essential is missing, and perhaps consider investigating within. But self-knowing is forbidden—and terrifying. Caught in unpleasant patterns, even deadly spirals, they feel incapable of changing. Lacking free will to choose in their best interest, they resign themselves to intensified allegiance to family, work and social tradition, no matter how deadening. Some use addictions and psychiatric drugs to buffer their pain.

***Rebels*—midlife rebellion, foes reconfigured**

> *Rebels* live in chronic crisis. In fact, they are addicted to it and often find themselves in a fix. However, at midlife some *Rebels* sense that things are amiss—that their rebellion hasn't brought them the peace for which they yearn. But what do they do about it? They have partial free will, but the options they see are to remain alive in rebellion by reconfiguring old foes or to die by returning to the lies of conventional society. Both leave them feeling empty and out of alignment with their deeper nature. That said, a rare few use the opportunity of the midlife crisis to wake up, look within and evolve into *Seekers*.

Seekers—midlife turning point

When *Seekers* face the midlife crisis, they come to a pivotal point of development. They can close their eyes and go the way of the norm or yet again go within. They have more free will than *Rebels*, because they have some connection with their true self. They make many good choices, which gives them more strength and more hope in life's promise. But their choice to be more real can be scary. This is to be expected. Going within requires great sacrifice—and there may be no going back.

Homo veritas—midlife deepens meaning

Homo veritas enter midlife understanding more deeply than ever that the answer to the human dilemma is within. They recommit more fully to live out of the best of who they are, because they lack a real choice—they are slaves to truth. With souls ablaze, they participate in all aspects of life, both internal and external, manifesting their gifts not only to fulfill their individual purpose but to serve the needs and nurture the growth of others. Every seeming choice they make affirms life's evolution toward truth and its quest for the sacred.

Psychosomatic Illness

Unresolved traumas in our psyche and anxieties from daily life can erupt in physical illness. Our bodies so easily bear the brunt of the conflicts we hold within. This is not to say that all human illness is psychosomatic, but a lot is or at least has a strong component. People at different levels of psychological evolution manifest psychosomatic illness as follows:

Homo sapiens—may manifest illness or not

Homo sapiens are psychically toxic. This leaves them at risk of developing psychosomatic illness. Instead of studying the illness's origin, they simply wish it gone immediately—and undergo surgeries or take medicines to bury the symptoms in the same way they bury their emotions. This process can be arduous and time-consuming, a perfect distraction for stuck people. Other *Homo sapiens* have so deeply buried the seed of their true self as well as its hurt and longing that they render themselves insulated from the psychic eruptions that cause psychosomatic illness. These are the *Homo sapiens* who live to be a hundred and beyond with seemingly perfect bodies.

Rebels—manifest illness as badge of honor

Rebels see illness as the price to be paid for the life of the outsider. They have lived hard, played hard and rebelled with intensity—all to feel alive and separate from the norm. They lack the ability to live in much comfort and become likely to manifest physically the unresolved trauma and blocked soulful yearning in their psyche. Many wear their psychosomatic illness as a badge of honor, an emblem of their defiance, an external proof that they really have suffered and continue to—even if they remain unaware that their real suffering is within.

Seekers—manifest illness, use as opportunity to grow

Seekers live so far outside the norm that life is stressful—perhaps even terrifying. Although they face their painful history, their traumas do not resolve overnight. Some manifest as illness, wreaking havoc on their bodies and offering them a choice: to fight the symptoms or resolve what is causing them. They use illness as an opportunity to self-study—to learn what is erupting and why. In this way, the illness itself provides a roadmap toward awareness.

Homo veritas—manifest health

Homo veritas are free of psychosomatic illness and are physically the healthiest specimens of humanity. Their wellbeing is assured by their alignment with truth. Since their unconscious is cleared of trauma, they don't need illness to speak for them or to them. They speak for themselves and to themselves from their core. If they do have an illness, it is not psychosomatic, rather, physical. After all, our bodies are physical entities that suffer wear and tear.

Mental Disturbances

When life's stressors combine with our buried traumas to overwhelm us, we risk manifesting mental disturbances. These can range from anxiety and depression to more extreme states like mania, delusions and voice hearing. These can negatively affect our feelings and our relationship to self and others. Yet these states can also present us with an opportunity to study ourselves, evolve and change our lives. But do we? The four types of humans relate to mental disturbances in the following ways:

***Homo sapiens*—emotions denied, drugged; numbness idealized**

> Most *Homo sapiens* in the western world view mental disturbances as biological or neurological diseases. They comfort themselves by saying their brains are broken and their neurochemicals are imbalanced. They believe in the sanctity of psychiatry and psychiatric treatment. They are quick to medicate their uncomfortable feelings with psychiatric drugs and other addictive tools—anything to bury their inner child's despair, rage and loneliness. Those who achieve a state of numbness and placidity are deemed normal—a state of insanity labeled ideal by the norm.

***Rebels*—emotions acted out but not processed**

> *Rebels* live on the emotional edge. They thrive on drama and continually reenact their childhood plight. They enjoy being a bit mad, even crazy, as part of their rebellious authenticity and fear the so-called sanity of the norm as a form of noncreative, psychic death. At times they may take pride in their mental problems and even wear their unhealthy behaviors and psychiatric diagnoses as a public identity. Perhaps they will take psychiatric drugs to manage their extremes, but they do not like the numb feelings and side effects that result—and often stop their drugs when the worst of the crisis has passed.

Seekers—emotions felt, investigated, healed

Seekers investigate their feelings and begin to recognize troubled emotions, even extreme ones considered insane by the norm, as symptoms of erupting childhood misery and need. They begin to appraise the full swath of the damage their parents inflicted on them and acknowledge how alone they were as children. But now they are not alone, for their developing adult self is present to parent the wounded child. This intrapsychic exchange between the adult self and inner child is the essence of self-therapy. An actual confrontation with birth parents may be useful, but is not necessary. Parents, if confronted, might once again deny the child's reality and retraumatize him or her.

Homo veritas—emotional wellbeing

Homo veritas perceive and experience reality correctly in its awe and majesty—and this defines sanity. They have experienced humanity's full emotional range, including grief at the tragic story of human history and also that which comes at the end of grief: joy in existence and reverence for life. They use all their faculties—feelings, intuition, reason and the senses—to venture deeper into a new creation. Life reassures them that growth, no matter how uncertain, will ensure a promising future, grounded in further emotional wellbeing.

Addictions

An addiction is a state of physiological or psychological dependence on a potentially harmful substance. That substance can be a drug or behavior and can be socially acceptable or unacceptable, depending on the mores and maturity of the society. The purpose of addiction is to divert and soothe painful, upwelling feelings—often from the past—into a seemingly comfortable alternative without allowing them to become conscious. In this way, addictions mute emotions and memories that are too disturbing to know and feel. Addiction keeps the mask of the false self in place and the true self hidden. The four types of humans relate to addictions in the following ways:

Homo sapiens—view addictions as physical diseases or normal

Homo sapiens turn to addictions to deaden the pain of childhood. They do not assess addictions' meaning, and at times don't even view addictions as addictions, rather, as something normal and healthy. At other times they view addictions as physical diseases. Regardless, the norm needs addictions to block access to their inner world. They use drugs, alcohol, sex, food, work, money, prestige, daily drama, family turmoil and, saddest of all, the creation of children, to numb feelings too painful to feel and to obliterate memories of perpetrators too difficult to name—especially mother and father.

Rebels—addictions resisted or glorified

Rebels have a mixed relationship with addictions. They glorify some addictive behavior as a testament to their struggle against repressive convention. Even the consequences of many addictions are seen as the price one must pay to be free from the norm. However, some addictions, such as that to heavy drugs, do trouble even *Rebels*, though rarely enough to provoke a comprehensive study into the addictions' deeper emotional underpinnings.

Seekers—addictions investigated to traumatic roots

As *Seekers* become increasingly aware of the underpinnings of their addictions, the story of their past emerges more clearly. They see the sorry tale of the child that addiction hid with deadening drugs and diverting behavior. They discern patterns in their acting out that were symbolic reenactments of actual traumatic events from childhood. They learn that they are not to blame for their sad childhood history, but are responsible to amend their addictive response to it. They also see that they are responsible to make amends to those they hurt—and that the best way to do this is to dry up their addictions at the source by healing their childhood wounds and properly meeting their historically unmet needs.

Homo veritas—awakened living, no addictions

Homo veritas engage in awakened living. Their inner child has been honored and nurtured, not muted by addiction or the allure of shortcuts, and has developed into the fullness of its adult capacity. In turn, this respected child blesses the adult with joy in existence and creative vitality. They avoid substances that others might find addictive, because they serve no purpose for them. They put healthy food and drink into their bodies and nurture their souls with love and tenderness. In this way they live clean, liberated lives.

Grieving

In order to grow people must grieve the loss of the old—their ancient history, their neglects, their traumas, their old self. Grieving is deep, intense, painful and propulsive. It shoots us out of depression and into the integration of the self. The four types of humans relate to grieving in the following ways:

Homo sapiens—grieving blocked

> *Homo sapiens* cannot grieve their deeper losses. Although some can grieve the death of a loved one, they fail to mourn their more primary losses—the loss of innocence, the loss of creativity and the loss of the true self from trauma. Being closed to their histories, *Homo sapiens* do not even know how much pain they are in. They are not even depressed, which is a precursor to grieving. Instead they are dissociated, living in a split-off bubble of comfort and conformity.

Rebels—stuck in perennial suffering

> *Rebels* admit that their parents and society hurt them and have some awareness that the false self of convention is a sham, but do not know how to deal with these losses. They cannot grieve and instead stay stuck in perennial suffering—a component of depression. To alleviate this they focus on external rage and blame—for they have discovered that anger makes an excellent quick fix for depression. They blame their parents and society for their despair, and yes, they're right, but external indictment can never heal internal wounds. Even if parents and society did admit everything, it wouldn't resolve childhood deficits.

Seekers—grieving the losses of childhood

With their broken-open heart, *Seekers* begin to feel the losses of childhood. This opens the doors of their suffering into the realm of grief. They no longer defend against the sad reality of childhood despair by maintaining a false self or winning the contest of life through grandiosity—or buffering their pain through depression. They indict those who harmed them and experience the child's anger and sorrow, feelings that would only have gotten them further abandoned when they were young. Now their inner child begins to feel relief as its story is heard, felt and integrated in the care of a capable and loving parent—their own adult self.

Homo veritas—grief has turned to joy

Homo veritas have fully grieved the tragedy of childhood and all its concomitant losses—and have entered the joy of existence as a new species. The adage is true: the greater the sorrow, the greater the joy. The inner child has matured from a wounded and half-hidden being into a self-aware adult who releases dynamic, creative energy. This energy evolves the consciousness of *Homo veritas* into realms unimaginable to the average and permeates all with whom they come into contact, prompting them toward further grieving, growth and awareness.

Relationship to Abusers

What relationship do we have toward those who caused us—and the world—harm? Do we despise them, chafe against them, forgive them—or understand them? And in what ways have we internalized their attitudes and behavior and become like them? And how do we treat those sides of ourselves? Our relationship to abusers, and the abuser within us, manifests quite differently in people at different levels of psychological development, as follows:

***Homo sapiens*—forgive family, deny own harm, blame others**

> *Homo sapiens* are quick to forgive their parents and other childhood authority figures the harm they caused, saying they did the best they could. Yet *Homo sapiens* don't even know the full extent of this harm, much less the effect it had on them. Thus their forgiveness is facile and premature—the bargain of a wounded inner child still seeking love and protection. And in a way this bargain works, because it brings them comfort. It keeps them welcome in the family system and gives them a future allowance to abuse others, including their own children. However, *Homo sapiens* are quick to blame others who are different from themselves, because they need them and even create them as an evil Other, a displaced outlet for repressed rage.

***Rebels*—blame norm, deny own harm**

> *Rebels* blame those who harmed them, especially their parents. They nurture grudges, feel the anger they were once not allowed to feel and are quick to confront. They are disgusted by forgiveness and mistrust those who promote it. However, they fail to see, much less explore, the ways in which they have become like their abusers—and how quickly they forgive themselves.

Seekers—healing the internalized abuser

Seekers' work is within and in order to do it they often take great distance from those who harmed them. Although they hold their abusers, chiefly their parents, accountable for their mistakes, they don't necessarily confront their parents, because they don't need their perpetrators' confession or contrition to heal. Instead they focus on healing their internalized abuser and strive to apply the eye of truth to the dark sides of themselves. They begin to understand that the harm they inflicted on others is a replication of the harm they endured. Through this they take responsibility for amending their own bad behavior—and simultaneously begin to forgive themselves.

Homo veritas—compassion for abusers, abhor the abuse

As wise parental figures, *Homo veritas* look with compassion and understanding on the destructive masses—wounded children. Although they abhor and condemn the atrocities, global and familial, that the human family has inflicted during its history, they understand the traumatic legacy motivating this bad behavior. This perspective allows them to love these lost children.

Facing Our Collective, Global Catastrophe

Our world is in serious trouble. The crises we ignore personally have gathered collectively into a global catastrophe—pollution, overpopulation, climate change, loss of species, war and economic collapse, to name a few. The four types of humans relate to this collective catastrophe in the following ways:

Homo sapiens—collective sleep

> Despite overwhelming evidence of the impending collapse of nature and society, *Homo sapiens* continue their lives as if nothing were wrong. They remain blissfully asleep. They continue to have children, bringing more innocent victims into this maelstrom. These children add their own strain on the environment, devouring limited resources and leaving more waste behind—and then they too have children, repeating the cycle. Like a mindless cancer, *Homo sapiens* are destroying the planet's ability to sustain life—including human life—a catastrophe they collectively ignore.

Rebels—collective nightmare

> *Rebels* wake up to a collective nightmare—and writhe in horror. They see the looming collapse of ecosystems and economies and are appalled at the damage we have wrought on ourselves and the world. They recognize that this disaster includes not only the extinction of so many plants and animals, but the looming extinction of humanity itself. They sound the alarm and work to save the planet and themselves from this global nightmare, yet lack the inner resources to cure it, because they do not face the cause—the unhealed inner world of our troubled species.

Seekers—collective awakening

Seekers awake to the realization that the planet's collective outer catastrophe reflects humanity's inner tragedy. They see that individual denial of trauma multiplied by the billions has caused a global economic and ecological cataclysm. They see the interconnection between the psychological microcosm of the individual and the physical macrocosm of society and nature. They work feverishly to heal themselves as a primary means to amend the world around them. They sense that individuals healing their childhood tragedy will add to the collective sanity of humanity and to a positive shift of consciousness. They just hope that it's not too late.

Homo veritas—collective consciousness

Homo veritas have fully awakened to the beauty and wonder of reality and themselves. Living consciously, they love our planet home—but not the insanity we have wreaked upon it. This they despise. But they do love what's best in others. They dedicate their lives to awakening the world to both the trauma and truth it carries in order to forestall and even turn around the collapse of nature and society. This is their mission and they work tirelessly to achieve it, living as proof that this new way, which they embody and radiate, is possible.

Chapter 5

The Interface of Ethics and Society

We interface with society through our relationships, our daily work, the expressions of our voice and the manifestations of our ethics. Our degree of emotional evolution impacts how we live in the world—and how we express our higher nature. Do we embody an ethical ideal, or do we exploit and harm?

- Ethics
- Our Voice in the World
- Working in the World
- Government
- Prosperity
- Commerce
- People's Attitude Toward *Seekers*

Ethics

Ethics are the code of morality by which we live. They are our determinants of right and wrong, good and bad, fair and unfair. Yet why do so many different people, and different groups of people, have such different codes of ethics? It may help to see that different people at different stages of emotional evolution relate to ethics in their own unique ways, as follows:

Homo sapiens—**lack internal ethics, follow external rules**

> *Homo sapiens* give lip service to ethics and may even believe themselves to be ethical, but in actuality follow the external rules of the culture as frightened, obedient children. They justify their crimes and compromises by saying they are following orders or obeying the law of the land or doing what their forefathers did, yet cannot see the ways in which they break the universal laws of truth. Cheated of an integrated self in childhood, they feel entitled to cheat to make up for this loss. They unconsciously feel that someone else should pay for what they lack inside.

Rebels—**whistleblowers, see corruption of society but not of self**

> *Rebels* fearlessly blow the whistle on the unethical ways of their parents, ancestors and culture—to the degree that they are aware of them. They are quick to voice their outrage and moral indignation at their forebears' lack of integrity, but fail to see their own lack of integrity—because they lack an integrated self. Since they remain fragmented, their ethics are situational and confused and not universal. They fail to see the full picture of issues, which leaves their battles for fairness narrow in scope.

Seekers—**begin to sort out ethics from within**

> *Seekers* begin to realize that their ethics, while an improvement over those of the norm, are partially flawed. They too lack

full inner integrity—a problem they are working on through grieving their childhood wounds. As their fragmented self comes together into wholeness, they begin to discover true ethics. As they align their outer behavior with their developing inner compass of right action, ethics become their guiding star.

Homo veritas—ethical living

Homo veritas live right and fear nothing. They are integrated within and live externally with integrity. They are guided by the universal principle of ethics, engendering justice, right action and fair play in all their doings. They are not ruled by fear and do not cheat. They live upright lives that succeed in ways unimaginable to most, yet provide others a yardstick for what all might someday be.

Our Voice in the World

A person's voice—not its sound but its essence—is a manifestation of his or her psyche, his or her connection with truth, his or her uniqueness of being. People at different stages of emotional evolution have different degrees of connection with their true voice in the world, as follows:

Homo sapiens—platitudes

> *Homo sapiens* lack their own voice and are instead the mouthpiece of convention. They imitate the voices of their wounding parents and culture and do not realize this. They cannot speak the language of truth, rather, they speak in platitudes and half-truths that accommodate and hide the lies, compromises and brutality of their upbringing. They are the voice of conformity. They may be witty, even seemingly wise, as they speak with words of collective comfort and compromise, but they do not speak the truth of the soul.

Rebels—rage, howl

> As *Rebels* leave their families and emerge from the prison of convention, they are full of rage and use their voice to howl in defiance. Their outbursts are raw and without definition, yet closer to the language of truth than those who raised them. As they rebel against the compromises of the conventional world, they explore the power, colors and notes of their forming voice. But something is out of tune—something is lacking.

Seekers—discover and articulate unique voice

As *Seekers* grow and heal they become more confident in their identity— and their voice reflects this. With a newer and truer sense of self, their painful utterances become articulate and nuanced. They find and define their voice. They're not yet fluent, but they're getting there. They're accumulating more practice in honest living and genuine communication, and increasingly the truth pours out of them—unfettered, uncensored and fearless. Their language becomes the language of authenticity, their voice a unique expression of their developing true self.

Homo veritas—voice of truth

Homo veritas speak with the clear voice of truth. Their words resonate with pure tone—rich and honest. They cannot tell a lie or embellish their voice with deception—nor do they wish to. Freed of trauma, they are a clear channel for honest speech, which surges through the unique colors of their personality. They are the human voice of the universe.

Working in the World

Work is the effort we put into life to obtain our food, our homes and our money. Work also provides many people structure to their days as well as a sense of purpose and meaning—or lack thereof. The four types of humans relate to work in the following ways:

Homo sapiens—exploit or be exploited

> As traumatized beings, *Homo sapiens* either exploit others or get exploited in their work. If exploited, they find this to be familiar ground, as it replicates their childhood patterns in which their existence was of little worth. As slaves, they may be hidden from view as illegal immigrants or underpaid workers in distant lands—or simply slaves to routine. If they exploit others, they take it as their turn to crack the whip and dominate as they were once dominated. Perhaps, though, like their parents they occasionally spread some beneficence—to divert from the reality of their cruelty.

Rebels—cut corners, attempt to beat the system

> *Rebels* are incensed by the corrupt and exploitative work practices of the norm. They react to this vice with undermining tactics. With self-righteousness, they cut corners to try to beat the system they hate. This may even be illegal by conventional standards, but at least they strive toward an open and honest call-to-accountability about the corruption of the ordinary. However, when they are in positions of power they often devolve into the very exploitative practices they despise—because their psychic template of unresolved trauma sets them up to do little different.

Seekers—doing inner work, which leads to vocation and mission

Seekers work in the world, but seek alternative, creative, non-exploitative ways to make a living. But their real work is healing their traumatic past, awakening their consciousness and manifesting their gifts. This can create conflict for them, as their outlook often contradicts the money-earning work systems of the norm. This tempts some *Seekers* to sell out, though many *Seekers* refuse this path, struggle financially, and do low-level tasks to pay bills. This leaves them free to do their real work—within.

Homo veritas—mission to awaken world

Homo veritas work to awaken the consciousness of the world. This is their job. They fulfill this mission through their unique gifts and talents—as expressed in their daily efforts. No matter their field of endeavor, from the mundane to the creative, their daily labor contributes to human enlightenment. They work as servants of life, truth and others.

Government

A government is a collective ruling power that makes and enforces the laws of a land. Governments can vary widely in their degree of emotional evolution, as they are affected by the degree of evolution of those who form them, as follows:

Homo sapiens—government as parental replacements

Homo sapiens choose leaders to lie for them, since they don't want the truth—chiefly the truth of their childhood. Politicians, presidents and kings pose as idealized parents, which is music to the ears of the unhealed masses. Some leaders promise rescue—the seeming nurture of a corrupted mother—through endless social programs to appease the unmet needs of childhood. Others promise revenge—the seeming strength and justice of the corrupted father—to express the rage of the lost, abused child. As in any dysfunctional family, the "mother" and "father" leaders blame each other for the trouble they're in. In more primitive cultures, tyrants, once brutalized as children, now become the brutal parents and wreak revenge on the populace they rule and countries they invade. All of this is familiar to the traumatized norm, which is why they allow for its perpetuation.

Rebels—anarchy, rebellion against authority

Rebels chafe against the deceptive authority and exploitation of governments and politicians. They do not trust any governments they have seen because they recognize them correctly as extensions of their own dishonest families. They cannot conceive of a government based on anything but force and untruth and they embrace anarchy as part of their rebellion. They work to radicalize others to join in dissent, defiance and civil disobedience, yet remain reactive to the old way.

Seekers—conceive of justice but focus on healing within

Seekers recoil in shock at the correlation between corrupt parents and corrupt politicians. As *Seekers* look within and heal their wounds, they begin to conceive of just forms of government that match their developing jurisdiction over their own psyche. As they become true leaders within themselves, they realize that inner healing is the prerequisite to reforming political systems. To this end, *Seekers* prioritize sharing their journey of healing over trying to change governments.

Homo veritas—enlightened leaders ruled by truth

In a world led by healed people, *Homo veritas* form a new system of enlightened government reflecting their embodied paradigm shift. The checks and balances for this new social order are their internalized ethical and altruistic standards. They use their authority for the benefit of all, because they realize that we humans, we living beings, we as a planet, are interconnected. They do not create a government of democracy where those who have the most children wield the most power. They realize that traumatized people cannot legislate public policy, because they are not equipped to make choices in even their own best interest, much less the interest of all. Unlike leaders of the norm, *Homo veritas* serve the public, leading them through a convulsive paradigm shift into conscious living—and ultimately true, cooperative civic responsibility.

Prosperity

Prosperity is abundance. It is the condition of having enough, be it enough money or property—as well as the less tangible things of life, like health, friendship, intimacy with others, connection with self and meaning in existence. The four types of humans relate to prosperity in the following ways:

Homo sapiens—never enough, always hungry for more

> *Homo sapiens* never got enough as children and bring this attitude of scarcity into adult living. They feel there is never enough money, food, property, power or love. Cut off from the fullness of their inner world, they are cut off from the abundance of life. Many go into debt financially—and all do emotionally, because they are spiritually bankrupt. Even if they accrue great wealth, they remain dissatisfied and want more. Simultaneously, they find comfort in others' poverty, because it deludes them into thinking themselves prosperous.

Rebels—hoarding to further rebellion or escape

> *Rebels* begin to feel the emotional riches and unfettered opportunities in their emancipation from the norm. But their sense of prosperity is based on external freedom and the perks of the outsider, not on the reality of internal abundance. This compels them to hoard wealth in order to further their escape from conventional constraint. For them, the means—at times destructive, even illegal—justify the ends of getting the loot needed for rebellious liberation.

Seekers—inner value discovered, external value redefined

Seekers work to feed their impoverished inner child and in so doing redefine prosperity as something that begins from within. This allows them to shun the old way of greed and compensatory materialism. They begin to pursue work that is fulfilling, even fun, irrespective of salary. They begin living for personal fulfillment and universal mission—not a paycheck or fattened bank account. As they heal the deprivation of their soul, they lose their need to go into debt and instead focus on that which they actually have. With this new perspective, they begin to see the degree to which they live in an abundant world of opportunity, ideas and limitless imaginative glee.

Homo veritas—abundant living from within

With a spirit-rich inner world, *Homo veritas* manifest the prosperity of external wellbeing. Cleared of trauma, they are fearless because there is more than enough within them and around them. In essence, they could live on air and be rich. They see reality as a cornucopia of awe-inspiring possibilities to be brought to fruition. An abundance of new ideas and inspired action flood through them.

Commerce

Commerce is the buying and selling of goods and services locally, nationally and globally. Commerce forms the basis of our local and world economies. Commercial practice reflects the level of evolutionary development of those who engage in it, as follows:

Homo sapiens—expanding markets on a limited planet

> With a greedy, frightened inner child, *Homo sapiens* rape the earth and exploit labor for short-term profit and long-term debt. They condone mindless population growth since this expands their markets, labor force and source of wealth. They think this system will work forever, but it won't. Instead they create a bubble where a few become rich and the rest scrape by, appeased by a glut of cheap goods and the false promise of better things to come. This addictive, unconscious approach to commerce, replete with unethical advertising, seeks to fill the hole of childhood deficits. But it is delusional, not just because childhood wounds can only be healed from within, but because the earth's resources are finite.

Rebels—oppose conventional business yet self-seeking in transactions

> *Rebels* are the whistleblowers of conventional commerce. They boycott businesses that overtly exploit people and natural resources. They refuse to be consumers of slave-made products that line the pockets of a few while destroying the natural world. They help raise consciousness and change unfair business practices of the norm, but remain unconscious of the neediness and rage of their own inner child. This leaves them self-seeking in their own commercial transactions—and unaware of how much they resemble the norm.

Seekers—begin to connect internal ethics with business ethics

Seekers go on strike inwardly against their historical exploiters. This is the most pressing business to which they must attend. As the result, they create alternative ways to sustain themselves both internally and externally, emotionally and financially. They work to find ethical and sustainable ways to provide services, manufacture goods and grow produce, just as they seek new ways to sustain themselves with self-nurture and self-protection. They strive not to cheat the rules of life—and investigate their inner selves if they note themselves going in that direction.

Homo veritas—conscious commerce

Homo veritas become leaders in the new field of conscious commerce. They enhance, not exploit, their fellow workers and the natural world. They promote education at all levels, so that people learn not only work skills but the human skills of self-respect and self-love. Since they are full within, they enter the world of business with a surplus—an abundant attitude and profound sense of gratitude for the bounty of life. Aligned with ethics, they treat others with the same respect and fairness they give themselves. As they prosper, so do others and the environment. Abundance is for all—and is everybody's business.

People's Attitude Toward *Seekers*

People at different levels of emotional evolution have markedly different attitudes toward people who engage in the process of resolving their traumas and begin to embody the best of humanity. How they relate to *Seekers* tells a lot about them, as follows:

Homo sapiens—shun them

> *Homo sapiens* are threatened by *Seekers*. *Seekers* upset the apple cart of their denial. *Seekers* shine a light on the norm's hypocrisy and danger and for this reason the norm despises them. But despising them openly is risky, so *Homo sapiens* take it a step further: they shun them. They attempt to nullify their existence by disqualifying their experience. Perhaps they neutralize them by labeling them insane, or perhaps they use corrupt laws to destroy them, their deeds and their reputations. *Homo sapiens* cannot dare risk taking *Seekers* seriously, because then they would have to take themselves, and their crying inner child, seriously.

Rebels—anxious around them

> *Rebels* are anxious around *Seekers* because *Seekers* take life a step further. *Seekers* fight for life, not against death, which shines a light on the smallness and limitation of rebellion. Thus, *Rebels* wish to push them away—yet at the same time are drawn to them. How could they not be? *Seekers* represent the life that *Rebels* only wish they could have—if they could just take another step forward, break away from the norm a bit more and start living for themselves. So in that sense *Seekers* are the not-quite-acknowledged role models for *Rebels*—objects of fascination but danger too.

Seekers—drawn to them

Seekers love other *Seekers*. They need peers on their lonely journey and have antennae out for others who dare to go within, confront painful truths and heal at all costs. *Seekers* have personalities meant to be around other brave souls who risk all to become true—and they enhance each others' lives. Sometimes, and in some places, *Seekers* are so rare that it might be decades before one comes across another. Many *Seekers* have long accepted a life of solitude, avoiding relational compromise, before meeting another *Seeker*. But now that is no longer necessary—and a new life of mutual growth and support can begin.

Homo veritas—guide them

Homo veritas respect *Seekers*—and provide them guidance through the pitfalls and agonies of healing childhood wounds and integrating split-off sides of the self. *Homo veritas* know all too well the anguish of growth and healing, having done it themselves, and share their surplus resources, both inner and outer, to help others in the process of waking up. *Homo veritas* see *Seekers* as a wise investment, because unlike *Rebels* and the norm, *Seekers* already have a strong connection with the truth of their inner selves.

Chapter 6

Our Relationship with Oneness

All things in the world are connected—in a sacred web of oneness. Humanity is connected to this oneness through our relationship with our true self. This chapter explores various ways we interface with this oneness—and how, to the degree we have failed to resolve our traumas, we miss out on this connection. Here we explore such themes as altruism, spirituality, art, enlightenment and being a visionary.

- Altruism
- Prayer and Meditation
- Envisioning a Better World
- Art We Create
- Attitude Toward Enlightenment

Altruism

Altruism is selflessness—an attitude or behavior marked by a concern for the welfare of others that is on par with one's love for oneself. However, people at different stages of psychological evolution love their own selves in markedly different ways, therefore have very different conceptions of altruism, as follows:

Homo sapiens—altruism denied, nepotism embraced

> Altruism is a foreign concept to *Homo sapiens*. Since they do not love their inner selves, they have difficulty loving others, nature and all that is. They see the world as fragmented and frightening: us-versus-them, us-versus-nature, us-versus-reality. They distrust those who differ from them and see nature as a force to be conquered—or ignored. Self-sacrifice, which they sometimes label as altruism, is limited to nepotism—family and parochial concerns. But even this is conditional, because the norm always expects something in return. Also, some confuse altruism with martyrdom, sacrificing themselves for others—often the very ones who abused them.

Rebels—altruism applied to fellow outsiders

> *Rebels* live perched on an island of isolation, thinking themselves different and hoarding their love. They shun identification with both the norm, whom they despise, and with *Seekers*, whom they fear. *Rebels* identify altruistically only with other outsiders. These are their friends, for whom they may even martyr themselves. Because they do not identify with their inner world, they cannot see their connection with the oneness of all things and thus cannot fully understand altruism.

Seekers—altruism awakens, begin to see universal commonality

As *Seekers* integrate their fragmented self into wholeness, they begin to see all of life as a sacred, interconnected web. As they integrate the best and worst in themselves, they begin to see that they are not so different from the best and worst in others. Through this they gain empathy and compassion for all things—and their altruism awakens.

Homo veritas—altruism embodied, life is an interconnected whole

Homo veritas are altruism embodied. They act for the benefit of all, and they start with their deepest selves. Yet they no longer belong to themselves, rather, to the universe, as its most evolved expression. Since their thoughts and actions affect all of reality, their individual lives have a universal implication—and they know this and cherish it. In this way, their private lives are paradoxically public, since they are connected to everyone and everything all the time.

Prayer and Meditation

In prayer, we speak to a different audience than we do in regular conversation. We speak to something beyond our daily limits, to a wiser, perhaps less known part of ourselves or the universe. In meditation, we quiet our mind to listen to the silent whispers of something else—perhaps something within, something beyond, something bigger or maybe smaller, quieter, more subtle. People pray and meditate in a variety of ways, depending on their level of psychological development, as follows:

Homo sapiens—rote and repetition

> *Homo sapiens* recite the prayers of their religious or cultural tradition by rote and repetition. They supplicate as needy children for selfish desires and alleviation of pain. At times they pray in grandiose, public display. They meditate by the rules of a guru for prescribed hours, sometimes chanting in mind-numbing repetition. They hope to quiet if not blot out their fears and desires—but never understand them. This is forbidden. Others don't pray or meditate at all, considering this inward dialogue an irrelevancy or simply an unreal musing.

Rebels—rebellious alternatives

> *Rebels* spurn traditional prayer and meditation as trappings of a convention that would soften their edge. They associate listening or talking to the god of their culture as analogous to appeasing or arguing with their dishonest parents. For guidance, some *Rebels* trust the rhetoric of other *Rebels*, whose points of view are rooted in indicting the average. This vital rant is a form of prayer. Other *Rebels* use drugs and alcohol to revel in altered states of consciousness, at times finding a meditative but non-transformative bliss. Others join religions from other cultures, praying and meditating through alternate forms which more often than not are little different from those of the norm.

Seekers—talk with and listen to inner depth

As *Seekers* begin to explore their inner world, they initiate an inner conversation. They may not call this dialogue prayer or meditation, but they discover that they can talk with and listen to their depth. This connects them to the maturity of universal meaning—and feeds their growth. When they speak in this dialogue, they express their concerns to their developing higher self, which responds with the guidance of a fuller perspective. When they listen to their inner self, they hear their core of truth, which reassures them that ultimately, beyond their day-to-day issues and beneath their unresolved trauma, all is well. Through this they find the strength to persevere.

Homo veritas—daily living is prayer and meditation

Homo veritas are always in a state of prayer and meditation. They talk with and receive guidance from the universal truth that surrounds them and courses through them. They hear the music of the universe and sing in harmony with it. They understand the universal thread of all spiritual traditions, yet see these traditions' limits in ways in which others, both followers and detractors, cannot. They live as an example that this thread can both be recaptured and woven into a fabric of ineffable wonder—and ordinary life.

Envisioning a Better World

To what degree can we envision a better world? Some people have a powerful ability to see beyond what is and imagine what might be. Others are limited in this. For this reason, some are visionaries and some are not. The four types of humans envision a better world in the following ways:

Homo sapiens—a blocked and traumatized vision

> *Homo sapiens* are blind to so much of reality that they find it impossible to imagine a significantly better one. Nor do they wish to. They see life as a battle to fight, a carnal prospect to exploit or even a disturbing nightmare from which to escape anesthetized, addicted, asleep. If they do imagine a new world, a new existence, they imagine one that meets their ideals—of more comfort, more people to meet their needs, more prosperity, less work and fewer responsibilities.

Rebels—a limited, distorted vision

> *Rebels'* outsider status has clued them in to a fuller picture of the world. They see visions of inexplicable horror, astonishing beauty and tantalizing wonder. Yet they do not follow the thread of what they have seen to its source within them. Their visions remain external, relying on adventures, fantasies and perhaps drug-induced highs to enhance their view of what might someday be. They avoid the inner work necessary to reveal the true magnificence of reality and stay stuck in a limited and conflicted existence.

Seekers—becoming visionaries

As *Seekers* journey into the inner wilderness, they encounter the raw psychic forces that allow them to imagine something new. Their imagination blossoms and connects with the truth flowing through all things. They start putting together the pieces of all they see and color it with creativity. They cannot help but become visionaries, but their primary vision remains focused on healing the unresolved sides of themselves, for that healing is their greatest gift to the world—and their most powerful source of originality.

Homo veritas—manifested visionaries living their visions

Homo veritas are manifested visionaries. They are able to see not only the consonance of reality, truth and nature, but the next level of being. They embody a sacred way of living to envision and generate a new creation, unfathomable to the average. Each day they walk a step closer to new wonders, only confirming to themselves and all of life our evolutionary progression.

Art We Create

Art is meaningful form created with skill and imagination. It can be expressed through various media and have a host of meanings and purposes. The art people create is an extension and expression of their mental and emotional development and their self-awareness and consciousness. It reflects their degree of social conformity, autonomous freedom, originality and authenticity, as follows:

Homo sapiens—diverting art

> The art of *Homo sapiens* is cultural propaganda, diverting attention from the inner world. It can be breathtaking in its beauty, chilling in its horror or clever in its amusement, but always deceptively quieting, lulling its audience into calm indifference to the calamity of the child's despair and buried magnificence. Although it denies the reality of childhood trauma, it gives expression to it indirectly. Unconsciously, the artist often portrays the wounded child's desire to be rescued and loved—through the metaphorical lens of sexual and romantic fantasy. Likewise, the artist may portray the child's rage and fear through violent and terrifying imagery. All of this safely alludes to the inner world, but never explicitly indicts those responsible for its disruption.

Rebels—iconoclastic art

> The art of *Rebels* is iconoclastic and irreverent, shattering conventional forms and seeking to radicalize the public. It indicts dishonest cultural and religious systems, but is ultimately self-indulgent. It feeds the neediness and rage of the inner child without taking responsibility for its healing. *Rebel* art is outer-directed, full of blame and recrimination. It repeats variations of the same theme, straining to be ever more outrageous and confrontational without daring to go within.

Seekers—exploratory art

The art of *Seekers* reflects the self-exploration of the artist. It discovers both the horror and wonder of ourselves—of humanity. It reveals the forbidden, shameful secrets of the family and encourages identification with the inner child's tragedy. Yet it also inspires the inner child's emancipation. As *Seekers* evolve they create transforming works of power and beauty that reflect their own inner growth—and the repressed beauty we all carry. *Seekers* are not indifferent to the message of their art, but rather learn from what they create—and strive to embody its lessons.

Homo veritas—life is art

The art of *Homo veritas* illuminates a new way of being human through its inspiration and instruction. It depicts a wondrous, never-before-seen reality, challenging assumptions and inviting all to see beyond old limits of imagination. It is a color of which people have never before conceived yet can feel in their core. It is a simple tone that rings true and beautiful. It is also embodied in their daily living—for their whole life is their art. As the old world collapses in crisis and catastrophe, their art is a message of hope and new meaning.

Attitude Toward Enlightenment

What is enlightenment? Generally speaking, enlightenment is considered to be a peak level of human psychological and spiritual development. However, people at different levels of emotional evolution view enlightenment through different lenses, as follows:

Homo sapiens—the enlightened are mystical, dissociated figures

Homo sapiens strive to be dissociated—to have all their trauma and pain and even joy split off in the unconscious—and envision the ultimate version of this as enlightenment. To them the enlightened being is a farfetched fantasy of a rare mystic, saint or all-knowing savior—disconnected from their own selves. This supposed being exists beyond the problems of the world—in a state of happy inner comfort, beyond criticism and pain and regret and perhaps even the laws of physics. This guru does not challenge them to look deeper at their childhood, but instead tells them that they too can enter bliss if only they can figure out how to dissociate more.

Rebels—the enlightened are idealized rebels

To *Rebels*, enlightenment is a state of perennial, selfless rebellion. They conceive of enlightened beings as those who risk their lives to criticize or sneer at the insanity of the norm and face exile to make a point. Such *Rebels* can change the world, because they carry a strong vitality and passion, but they don't inspire people to go within. In fact, like the norm, they inspire the opposite.

Seekers—becoming enlightened

For *Seekers*, enlightenment is the dissolution of the unconscious. When traumas heal, the unconscious disappears—and the channel of truth opens up. *Seekers* realize that they are becoming enlightened—day by day, piece by piece, with every trauma they grieve and every new bit of truth they comprehend and integrate.

Homo veritas—enlightened beings

Homo veritas are enlightened beings—connected at all levels. They interface directly with truth, which flows into them, through them and out of them again. Yet they know this state is no end in itself. Their enlightenment is not a ticket out of the world, but a passage into it and its darkness. *Homo veritas* enter the fray of troubled humanity to bring them the transforming light of truth. And their work is not done until all have seen this light within—and taken up its torch.

Chapter 7

The End of Life

As we near the end of our lives, we have the opportunity to assess the results of our choices and determine how they have influenced our journey. Have we become wise? Are we aging gracefully? Have we contributed to humanity's development to the utmost of our potential? Where have we succeeded? And where have we failed? As we approach death, the questions of life's meaning and transcendence have the potential to become central, even primary. But do they?

- Attitude Toward Aging
- Suicide
- Wisdom
- Death and Dying
- Our Legacy
- The Destruction of Our Environment
- Who Will Survive?

Attitude Toward Aging

How do we deal with growing old? Will these be our golden years or bitter days? Will we share what we've learned or keep it to ourselves? Some people accept aging, some fight it and some embrace it. And for some it is a profound crisis that creates a major paradigm shift—perhaps for better, perhaps for worse. The four types of humans relate to aging in the following ways:

Homo sapiens—regression into comfort or decrepitude

Homo sapiens face their aging in a variety of ways. Those who have built enough of a protective wall of comfort around themselves regress to the lives of satisfied, selfish children, even infants, letting others take care of them and their whims. Their attitude says, "Let the descendants be bitter and weary—they will have their day; my day is now." Other *Homo sapiens* are not so lucky—if they haven't padded their lives so effectively. They must face the ugly reality of life's consequences and they don't like it. Some age into bitterness and decrepitude—while others experience a paradigm shift and become *Rebels*, turning their backs on their long-held attitudes and goals and leaving themselves unrecognizable to those who have long known them.

Rebels—bitter rebellion

Rebellion against aging is not pretty, because you cannot win. *Rebels'* bodies and minds don't work as well—nor do their psychological defenses. *Rebels* can no longer keep their lies and traumas so easily at bay. Also, it's hard to keep diverting their anger and rage and unmet needs toward an external enemy when their mortality is staring them in the face. For this reason *Rebels* resent old age and blame the world for it. They become like neglected children—selfish, hurt, unstable, desperate for love yet not quite trusting. They often push away, even alienate, those trying to help them. Some *Rebels*, however, undergo a major paradigm shift here, giving up their rebellion and regressing into the comfort of the norm.

Seekers—seeking to the end

Seekers have mixed feelings about aging. The parts of them connected with their true self feel satisfied. They see how they have lived lives of value, have come to know themselves better and have made something special of their existences. Yet they still have unhealed parts, unmet needs, unseen hurts. To this end, they explore life's meaning with vigor. They study themselves more, work to grieve more ancient hurts and tie up loose ends. They realize this is their final chance to put in the labor to evolve, and so, rather than rest on their laurels, they buckle down and look forward, into a new future.

Homo veritas—fountains of youth

Homo veritas age well. The fountain of youth is a freed spirit, a harvest of wisdom and joy. Many years lived consciously creates the sage—someone able to teach the young the sweetness of life. They do not hide their age for they have earned their wrinkles and grey hair through the stress of expanding truth and living responsibly. A youthful glow emanates from their being for all to see. Many wonder, "What does this person have?" Their spirit has not been crushed by a burden of unresolved trauma. Their ally is life—not death. Their spirit is ageless and eternal—and in a sense so are they.

Suicide

Suicide is the act of deliberately killing yourself. People end their lives by suicide for a variety of reasons. But who are the most susceptible, and why? The four types of humans are at risk of suicide in the following ways and commit suicide for the following reasons:

Homo sapiens—all of life is suicide, some actually commit it

> Like anyone trapped in a lie, *Homo sapiens* are susceptible to suicide. With childhood trauma pushing up and denial pushing down, this pressure cooker risks becoming volatile. If the mix explodes, it pushes some over the tipping point. It is do or die—tell the truth and get real or end it all. For many *Homo sapiens*, getting real is out of the question. Similarly, life's vicissitudes—a failed venture, a failed love relationship, lingering hopelessness, physical disability or pain—can throw *Homo sapiens* into a suicidal crisis. And why not? Secretly they have been suicidal since they made their first psychic choice in life and gave up their healing process in order to walk the norm's path of psychic death.

Rebels—reckless living is an expression of suicide

> *Rebels* know their lifestyle has a daredevil side to it. They find this more alive than the deadening corridors of convention. Yet within this recklessness lives a death wish, since the path of rebellion also avoids the integrating journey to life. In that sense *Rebels*, like *Homo sapiens*, commit suicide their whole lives. Some, however, take it a step further and end their physical lives. They do so when rebelling fails, when joining the norm feels worse than death and when growing and facing their inner demons is too terrifying.

Seekers—suicide an option, but decide to take their lives seriously

Seekers contemplate suicide. It looms as a choice, because healing can be so painful and lonely. In a dark moment, some consider ending it all. But curiosity at life's possibilities intercedes and they pause. They endure another moment, another hour, another day, sensing that a way will appear if only they don't give up. Life always found a way in the past, a way through and out. Their wisdom has taught them that circumstances change and evolve in ways they never thought possible. Through this, life's promise is restored, even when all seems lost. Thus, a *Seeker* does not take his or her own life—but decides to take it seriously, and take it to the next level.

Homo veritas—never commit suicide, choose life

No matter the hardships or mental anguish of enlightened living in a corrupt world, *Homo veritas* choose life and live for truth. They are not tempted to do otherwise. They honor the gift of life and its unfolding, deepening odyssey. They know that life is a gift not to be squandered and they never commit suicide—even if their bodies are giving out from physical pain. They know that all circumstances, even the heartbreaking, can be used for good—for soul growth and the evolution of consciousness. They understand that the most difficult times give the most precious gifts, the life lessons that burnish the treasures of wisdom.

Wisdom

Wisdom is good sense, an ability to make mature decisions and judgments. Later life is the most logical time to have accrued wisdom. We have lived longer and have more life experience—and have had more time to integrate our personal insights with universal truth. This does not mean, though, that all people develop an equal amount of wisdom, as follows:

Homo sapiens—wisdom is accepted dogma, blind faith

> *Homo sapiens* shy away from personal insight and do not process their life experience. This makes them unable to access innate wisdom or generate new wisdom. Instead, they accept the wisdom handed down from their parents and ancestors—and have difficulty questioning it, no matter how wrong it is. When they are in doubt or troubled, they turn with blind faith to the collective dogma held in familial, social or religious tradition. Even if these learned truths never answered their deepest yearnings nor quieted their upwelling pain, they refuse to investigate further.

Rebels—wisdom is defiance of dogma

> *Rebels* see that traditional wisdom and religion never resolved humanity's deepest concerns, nor ended humanity's penchant for greed and violence. They see that this dogma led many down a passive, infantilizing path. But they don't see much further. They remain reactive to these failed teachings, yet unable to forge new ones. Their wisdom is their intuitive defiance—though they tend to defend it with seemingly rational arguments.

Seekers—gaining real wisdom

Seekers ask life's questions and receive answers from within. Having processed the data of so much life experience, they have accumulated a wealth of insight—true wisdom. With other *Seekers* they refine and expand their discoveries. They take delight in sharing what they have learned and others come to recognize them for their wise ways. But part of their wisdom involves self-critique—because they know that as long as they live with some trauma within, their perceptions still contain the seed of distortion.

Homo veritas—embody and expand wisdom

Homo veritas embody wisdom—and this treasure trove of insight increases as they continue to evolve. As trauma-free vessels, they find truth surging through their human matrix. This generates new depth and new perceptions—wisdom at a whole new level. These insights deepen the understanding they have already developed—which ultimately expands the meaning of truth itself.

Death and Dying

There is a finite length to our journey on Earth. One day we will all die. However, people at different stages of evolution face their own death and dying differently, with different levels of awareness, maturity and acceptance. The four types of humans face their process of death and dying in the following ways:

***Homo sapiens*—struggle to avoid dying an abandoned child**

> The worst fear for *Homo sapiens* is to face death alone—as abandoned, forsaken children, unparented even by themselves. Since they have not healed their traumatic past, they live at risk of having all they have avoided for a lifetime coming back to confront them in a tidal wave. They do all they can to avoid this end—in hopes of sliding out of life blissfully unaware. Some lose their minds to dementia as an attempt to blot out everything. Others relish the opportunity to die drugged on painkillers, ostensibly to numb their suffering bodies but actually to numb their aching, terrified and now erupting inner child. Others die dissociated—surrounded by family members and even religious leaders lulling them into the delusion that all will be okay, they're going to a better place and all they have to do is let go.

***Rebels*—try to cheat death, fight to the end**

> *Rebels* die awash in the pain of their upwelling inner child. Their rebellion against the norm stymies them from using conventional tools to buffer themselves against the inner reality they never investigated. And so *Rebels* face their final rebellion: trying to cheat death. Some deny outright that they are dying, never intellectually or emotionally acknowledging what is happening to them and instead using bitterness and rage to control the horrifying fear brewing within. Others become overwhelmed by these erupting feelings, lose their minds and are rendered terrified children, even infants. Others devolve into

Homo sapiens and try to blot it all out. Perhaps a few wake up and become *Seekers* at the end, but this is unlikely. Most people who spend a lifetime avoiding something have little ability or strength to face it at the end.

Seekers—strive to seek to the end

Seekers die facing a great challenge: to continue doing what they have long struggled to do—to hold their inner child in their adult care, protection and comfort. It is a challenge to do this at this most vulnerable and painful time. Some become overwhelmed with grief at the tragedy of all they have left undone and give up, while others seek right up to the end.

Homo veritas—die into the next chapter of life

Homo veritas die consciously—and their worn-out bodies match the completion of their earthly mission. Their inner child has developed into a fully self-aware adult who perceives dying as a transition from one level of meaning to another. *Homo veritas* intuit that death is not the end, but a profound extension of existence. This they face with courage and curiosity, since its mystery has always been part of the daily mystery of life. They sense that there is more to come, an afterlife of some kind of which they will be a part, since they have always been united with all that is and has been. With gratitude they remember their lifetime of opportunities, bid farewell to this magnificent planet and die at peace—for that is how they have lived.

Our Legacy

When we die, we leave a legacy. It might be money or property, it might be our artistic projects, it might be our ideas, it might be our children and it might be whatever traumas we have not resolved and have instead passed on. And it also might be nothing, as this is a reality for some people. It all depends on our degree of emotional evolution, as follows:

Homo sapiens—catastrophe

Homo sapiens leave a legacy of an overpopulated, polluted planet. Instead of healing ancestral trauma, most had children and had too many, passing on their wounds and unmet needs to the next generation. They've littered the world with mountains of garbage, toxicity, radioactive waste and troubled descendants. They've decimated countless species of plants and animals, many of which are now extinct. They leave a world of technological gadgets, advanced weaponry, brutality and war. Their extinction looms ever closer, as a logical outcome of their unconscious patterns. And in spite of their unconsciousness, at some level they know it.

Rebels—rebellious struggle

Rebels leave a legacy of rebellious struggle. They have put their lives on the line again and again in their battle against the steamroller of the norm. They remained true to their raw impulses and leave their mark as ones who survived as outsiders, pariahs and misfits. Their goal was to unclog the constricted channel of conventional compromise and open a new way, and to some degree it worked. But since they never changed their inner selves, their legacy is limited.

Seekers—courageous self-exploration

Seekers leave a legacy of courageous self-exploration. They have entered the inner wilderness, beyond the borders of their limited families, and share what they learned. They inspire others to go within, search out the roots of family and societal trauma and embark on the journey toward truth. With their shining souls increasingly reclaimed from repression, they mutate into a new way of being and leave their ongoing process of healing as a hopeful possibility for all who remain in darkness.

Homo veritas—new consciousness

Homo veritas leave a legacy of new consciousness. By leading enlightened lives they have redefined what it means to be human. Through the daily discipline of an alignment with truth, they have generated a new prototype for humanity that ripples through the universe. Their lives have caused a paradigm shift in awareness that all can feel. Even in quiet solitude, they affected global consciousness. Their legacy is the growth they induced and nurtured, the love they gave to themselves and others and the wisdom they taught and embodied. They have etched new meaning in the book of life through their existence.

The Destruction of Our Environment

The environment of Earth is presently being destroyed and our world as we know it is facing its end. Whole ecologies are being disrupted beyond repair, species are being driven extinct at a rate hitherto unknown and pollution is rampant to the point of making our planet toxic for everyone and everything. And humans are largely to blame for this. The four types of humans view this destruction differently, as follows:

Homo sapiens—blind or myopic

> The norm is blind to what is happening on the planet, and if they are aware, which they are increasingly becoming pressured to do with the worsening environmental catastrophe, they see the problem myopically, to be solved through clever technological invention. Most remain oblivious, lost in their bubbles of personal existence. They care only about their own needs, their own special interests and most importantly the maintenance of their own comfort. They do not care that their children will someday have to face an even more catastrophically destroyed environment, because they never had children for their children's sake; they had children for self-gratification. And that, ultimately, is how they view the whole world: there for them.

Rebels—blaming others

> *Rebels* realize that something terrible is happening on our planet and blame the norm—and want to change the norm to make things better. Perhaps they realize that human overpopulation is a central part of the problem, but they don't know what to do about it. Ultimately, they love nature in the same way they love themselves: in fragments. It is impossible for them to consider that they failed to do the one thing that would provide the best balm for the world—inner healing. Instead they seek outer solutions, such as technology or surface change, if they seek

any at all. Oftentimes it is easier for them to avoid the global problems of the world and focus on small parts of it—certain issues within the greater problem.

Seekers—aware and appalled

Seekers are appalled by what is happening to the environment. They see that the horror in what we are doing to our planet's ecology is an external manifestation, writ large, of the horror in family systems and within those who are not fully healed. They abhor the worshipful misuse of technology and see the waste it generates on the planet and the distance it puts between people, their souls and the earth. Their awareness of this propels them forward into healing the ecology over which they have the most control: their inner world. But they never stop looking at the outer world. Healing is not just within—it just happens to start there.

Homo veritas—aware and mobilized

Homo veritas are aware of what is happening on our planet and it horrifies them. Having healed their inner wounds, they use their energy to help others heal, because they recognize that unhealed people can do little, if anything, to assist the environment in its healing process. *Homo veritas* also live as models for others—eating sustainable foods, living within their means, not having children on an overpopulated planet and being public and outspoken—in a firm but gentle way—about their life choices and their reasons for making them.

Who Will Survive?

How sustainable are different varieties of human beings? Who among us will stand the test of time, and how? The sustainability of the four types of humans differs notably from one type to the next, as follows:

Homo sapiens—unsustainable

Homo sapiens are unsustainable. Theirs is a history of a powerful people who ensured their survival through procreation and violence. Now they swarm the planet like a cancer and destroy life at every turn. Unhealed of their traumatic legacy, their fate is to manifest large, violent and unconscious populations that clog the planet's ability to sustain life—including human life. They have survived thus far because the world, in its immensity, has been able to absorb their mess. But that time has ended. The polluted environment mirrors their toxic, deadly and denied inner world. The poison with which they pollute the planet pollutes them as well. If left unchecked and if unhealed, *Homo sapiens* will destroy themselves, choking on their own negativity and garbage.

Rebels—unsustainable

Rebels fled their fear-based families because they could not survive that deadening environment. But they did not find a new way, and because of this are unsustainable. They entered the wilderness to save their enlivened spirit but failed to evolve to a higher level of self-awareness. Ultimately they are just a reaction to the norm, not a sustainable, new prototype. Their vision and voice are derivative, not original, and in the sweep of things they differ little from those against whom they rebel.

Seekers—becoming sustainable

Seekers are on the path to sustainability. In the parts of themselves where they have resolved their traumas and become true, they are sustainable. And in the parts of themselves that still play out traumatic childhood patterns, they are not. Ultimately trauma is not sustainable, and no one who carries it is. That is why *Seekers* are a transitional type of human—leading us toward the next species of humanity. They are not quite there yet, but have all the building blocks to make it.

Homo veritas—sustainable

Homo veritas are sustainable. With a fully integrated self that honors natural law, they are aligned with the truth of life, the planet and the universe. They embody a new paradigm for being human and help others do the same. They not only survive but thrive and manifest and continue to evolve consciousness into new levels of meaning. Their lives become sacred, nurtured and protected by universal forces. They are the future of evolution, the hope of the world and the stewards of the next era.

Conclusion

As I conclude these pages, I ask myself what gives me hope. In these troubling times it is easy to lose faith in humanity and live instead for distraction and comfort. My first answer is that I believe there are a lot of us out there who are open to this message. I sense there are many *Seekers* in the world—many living in solitude in the midst of the norm, but many others slowly coming together and joining forces. We are becoming a conscious community, and this community is growing.

This is the basis for a profound change in the world, which brings me to my second answer about what gives me hope: that I myself have changed. I have evolved—and am still evolving. I am becoming more fully myself. I was born different, a mutation in some fundamentally positive way—and I have done something with it. Meanwhile, I would guess that if you are reading this, you too were born different.

Third, I have hope because I see myself releasing more of my gifts. This book is one of them—and also a consequence of my healing, of my evolution. And it too evolved over the seven years that I wrote it. It became shorter, more direct, more honest, even more artistic. I did my best to boil it down to its essence, which scared me, both because I feared it would lose something important—and that it wouldn't: that it would actually say, without distraction, what I intended to say. And I think it has.

By sharing this field guide I believe I am contributing not just to our evolution but to the evolution of nature—because our evolution, the evolution of even one human nature, contributes to the evolution of all. And although I cannot deny the catastrophe I see happening around us, I retain hope in the knowledge that nature is more powerful than our hubris, truth more powerful than lies, grieving more powerful than trauma and a sane few more powerful than the traumatized masses. This gives me the deepest hope.

The End—or the Beginning

Edwards Brothers Malloy
Thorofare, NJ USA
March 23, 2016